The Third Year
of Life

The Early Childhood Development Center's Parenting Series

The Third Year of Life

Nina R. Lief, M.D.
with Rebecca M. Thomas

Walker and Company ☀ New York

First published in the United States of America in 1991 by Walker Publishing Company, Inc.

Published simultaneously in Canada by Thomas Allen & Son Canada, Limited, Markham, Ontario

Library of Congress Cataloging-in-Publication Data
Lief, Nina R.
The third year of life / by Nina R. Lief with Rebecca Myers Thomas
p.   cm. —(The Early Childhood Development Center's parenting series)
Includes bibliographical references and index.
ISBN 0-8027-1155-3. —ISBN 0-8027-7351-6 (pbk.)
1. Parenting.   2. Child development.
3. Toddlers.   I. Thomas, Rebecca Myers.   II. Title.
III. Series.
HQ755.8.L533   1991
649'.123—dc20   91-13038
CIP
Rev.

Printed in the United States of America

2   4   6   8   10   9   7   5   3   1

For
Brooke and Austin Thomas
and
all the children who have participated in the
Early Childhood Development Center's program
and all the children to come.

Contents

■   ■

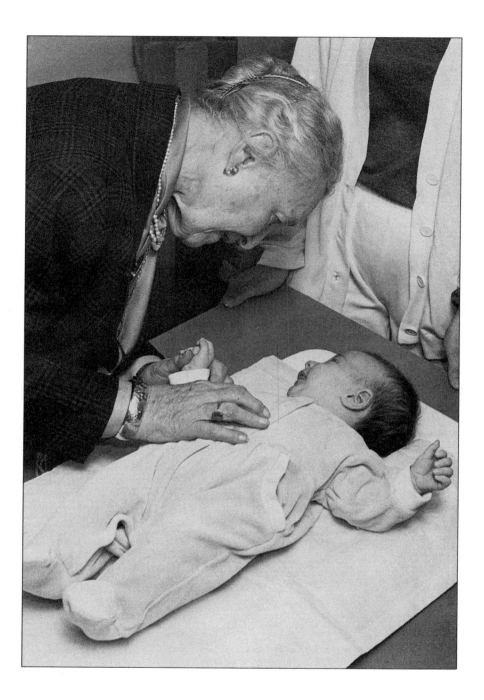

Much research has been done on the crucial importance of a child's earliest years, but little of the knowledge and understanding derived from this research reaches the parents, who have primary responsibility for the child's care and development. To provide parents with this information as well as with support and encouragement in their roles as parents, New York Medical College and the New York Junior League established the Early Childhood Development Center in 1974.

At the Center, small groups of parents (usually from eight to ten adults) and their children meet with a trained group leader in weekly discussion sessions. The curriculum for the discussions is based on the best current information regarding a child's emotional, social, and cognitive development, as well as on the real-life concerns of parents, as expressed in their questions. The links between appropriate childbearing methods and developmental theory are continually demonstrated, thereby enabling parents to see how child-rearing techniques directly influence the child's cognitive, social, and emotional development.

The major aims of the Center's program are to assist parents in guiding their children toward healthy personality development and to help mothers and fathers derive enjoyment and satisfaction from their roles as parents. While other programs have emphasized the physical and cognitive aspects of a child's development, the Center is more concerned with helping the parent understand the emotional and social side of that development and the importance of parent-child interaction in this process. The Center recognizes the uniqueness of each child and each family's situation. It adheres to the belief that the most effective child rearing results from the parents' understanding of their own child's needs, temperament, and level of development as well as knowledge of appropriate child-rearing options. Parents come to understand and follow the child-rearing practices appropriate for their own child through the discussions at the parenting sessions rather than from specific directions, as no one method suits all children.

The curriculum used at the Early Childhood Development Center has been published in three paperback volumes: *The First Year of Life; The Second Year of Life;* and *The Third Year of Life.*

This book is divided into two sections covering the third year of life in six-month intervals. Each of the chapters focuses on developmental highlights followed by the discussion, as it took place with parents at the Early Childhood Development Center, of a series of topics relating to child development and child-rearing issues, as well as parents' feelings.

Every effort has been made to avoid sexist use of pronouns in referring to the gender of the children who form the subject of this book. This explains why the pronoun referring to the child is sometimes masculine and sometimes feminine, and why the gender of the pronoun appears to change arbitrarily from section to section.

Similarly, throughout the text the parent is more often referred to as the mother, rather than the father. This is not due to any sexist orientation but simply to the fact that the great majority of the parents who provide the major amount of care during the child's earliest years are mothers. It is our belief that parenting is a shared male-female responsibility, and the word "father" may be substituted for the word "mother" in most cases.

Further, a growing number of mothers of children under three years of age are working outside the home. Because the child's needs regarding nutrition, attention, and discipline are similar whether his or her parents work, topics throughout the book discuss the variety of ways that parents in differing circumstances may meet their children's needs. This is important and possible, whether parents work outside the home or not. The purpose of this book is to foster the healthiest possible growth and development of the child and to make parenting less stressful and more enjoyable.

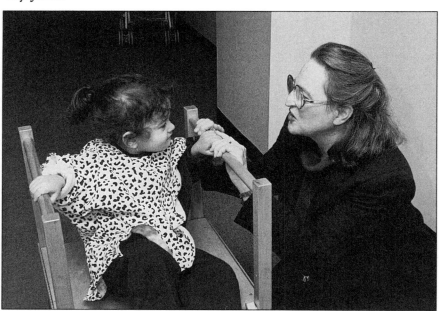

■   ■

The Third Year of Life

SECTION I

Age Twenty-four to Thirty Months

*T*he child's second birthday is one with special significance for parents. There has been tremendous development over the past year. At the beginning of the year, some of the children were walking with one hand held; a few were toddling on their own. Now most of them run with little or no falling. They can also negotiate stairs alone, both up and down, some even without holding on to the railing. They can kick a large ball upon request without demonstration. When interested in looking at a book, they can turn the pages singly.

At one year, the children could sometimes make a tower of two blocks after demonstration by the parents. Now the children can build a tower of six or seven blocks without demonstration. They can also align two or more blocks into a "train."

The two-year-old no longer scribbles when clutching a crayon in his hand; he may be able to imitate a V and circular stroke. Now when a puzzle with simple geometric shapes is presented, the child may put all the pieces in place after several attempts, indicating that he has learned to associate shapes. He can also insert the square block into the perform-ance box, instead of just inserting the corner, as he did three months ago.

Most children have progressed from the three or four single words they knew at one year to many phrases and two- and three-word sentences. They may even have discarded jargon, the imitative sounds made before words and meaning become associated. They may even use the pronouns "I," "me," and "you." The children may be able to refer to themselves by name and verbalize an immediate experience, as well as ask for "more" or "another."

The children have also made great progress in their social develop-ment. They are now able to eat with a spoon without turning it over, although finger feeding may still be preferred and eating may still be quite messy.

While dressing, they may be able to pull on simple garments such as underpants, pants, or an open sweater, often with the arms in backward. And they may indicate their preferences for special items of clothing.

All of the above tasks are preparing them for a major step forward—

gaining autonomy. The two-year-old is progressing from being an infant to a separate person. In what ways will they achieve autonomy and how will parents be able to help them? These are some of the questions we will answer in this book.

In the next six months, parents can expect the children to exercise more and more independence. The children may wander away from the parent more frequently, ask a parent to do things their way, demand to sit in a favorite chair, or issue commands for parents to obey. Understanding why and how a child does these things will enable the parent to traverse the treacherous territory often referred to by others as the "terrible twos." If the parent is able to keep in mind that the emerging individual is just practicing and refining his technique, life becomes more amusing and less anxiety-ridden and confrontational.

■

Your Child's Progress

The children have made enormous progress in the last year—they have gone from crawling to walking and now running. They are taking on their own  unique personalities, yet they are still very young and immature. We have noticed that parents' expectations of their children are sometimes beyond the child's level of development. Occasionally, parents are unaware of the progress their child has made and do not enhance it by recognition. Are there some achievements you were expecting by now that haven't occurred? Are you surprised at things your child doesn't do yet?

"I've been looking forward to conversations with my son, but although he seems to have a pretty big vocabulary and knows the names of most things, he doesn't make sentences yet. I'm getting a little worried. Am I expecting too much too soon?"

Most children do not speak in sentences until the age of three. They begin to say short phrases by two and a half, such as "Mommy, bye bye" or "Daddy car" instead of "Mommy is going away," "Daddy is going to the car." Some may be more verbal than that. Each child's development goes at his own maturational pace. Most children, but not all, use short sentences by age three. Some seem to say very little for a long time, and then are able to express themselves well all at once.

"Being able to talk with our child is the most important area of growth for us. Is there any way to hurry it?"

We can't change endowment for speech development. However, speaking to the child and modeling clear, modulated speech can help stimulate speech, while a barrage of unmodulated speech may retard it. For example, when giving a child juice one mother may say, "Here is Johnny's juice," emphasizing juice while enunciating clearly and speaking slowly. That is helpful to the child.

Another mother may say quickly in a monotone, "Here's your juice, Johnny. Drink it all up, because it's good for you and Mom wants you to be healthy." This is well-intentioned, but it is too much all at once and makes it difficult for the child to pick out the key word. He may understand his mother's interest, but the individual words do not stand out for him.

"Is it too much to expect children of this age to put toys back in place? I have tried by showing my daughter, but she doesn't seem to catch on and do it often."

Parents can show children where things go—the shoe goes here, the block goes there, garbage goes here, and hats go here. When they put something away, parents should recognize the action. When children do something that pleases a parent, they want to do it again and again. And when Daddy comes home, you can say, "Do you know what Amy did today, she put her slippers in the closet."

"Every time they do it? Even if they have done this particular thing several times and they know that I notice it?"

After constant recognition and approval from parents, children internalize the recognition and don't need it from anyone else. The adults who need the most recognition are the ones who received the least when they were children. Constant approval of acceptable behavior is what regulates children's motives and develops their self-esteem.

"I'm expecting my son to accomplish toilet training in the coming year. My mother and husband think that I should have begun toilet training long before this, but I didn't feel my son was ready."

Children indicate readiness for toilet training. The child has to be able to recognize the sensation of pressure in the rectum or bladder, communicate this to his parent, withhold expulsion until placed on the toilet, and then relax his sphincters. This is a complicated process. Most children demonstrate readiness for it by the end of the third year. Forcing toilet training on a child usually slows down the process and often sets up an angry relationship between parent and child, with disappointment for both. Some experts believe that this relationship may carry over into adult life and affect personality development. Because of the importance of this issue, it will be dealt with in many of our sessions.

"I would like my daughter to be able to let me out of her sight once in a while and play by herself. She always seems to want to be close to me."

Children need to be close to their parents, particularly mothers, for much longer than adults think necessary. The child can run off from mother because he knows that he will come back. But when mother leaves, he does not have assurance that she will return. The more parents try to push separation before the child is ready, the more the child will cling.

By the end of the third year children are able to separate from parents more easily. However, in times of stress, such as going to nursery school, they may need their parents' presence until they feel more secure.

■   ■

"How long do we have to put up with the mess during meals? My husband doesn't want our child to eat at the table with us until he learns to eat properly."

By age three, most children can use a spoon and a fork adequately, although they may still use a fist grip most of the time. Occasionally, they will still assist their spoon feeding with some hand feeding. Parents should not expect children to be able to eat neatly until they are well past three.

"My husband, too, gets upset by the messy eating. Because he thinks table manners are very important, he scolds and corrects our child whenever we eat together."

Table manners are better taught by modeling than by scolding. When children are ready, they need only a little help in holding utensils properly—and approval when this is accomplished—to begin establishing table manners.

"I'm worried because my child eats so little. I understand that there is a falling off of the appetite in the second year, but when is it regained?"

By the middle or end of the third year, most children regain their appetites. However, a few children continue to do very well on a small intake. Parents of these children may become anxious and try to force food. This is never productive; it may inhibit a child who, left to his own timetable, would have begun to eat more.

"I'm still waiting for our daughter to sleep through the night. Of course, she used to wake several times a night. Now she wakes at least once, sometimes twice, and needs a drink of water or just some reassurance. She goes back to sleep quickly, but I haven't learned to do that yet!"

Some children are always good sleepers. Others are easily aroused during sleep by any number of things, such as a noise, thirst, a gas pain, a dream, fatigue, even anticipation of something pleasant like a promise of a new toy. Wakefulness may become a life-long characteristic, but as children get older, they can cope with it on their own and don't require a parent's presence. Perhaps during this year a better sleeping pattern may be established.

"My child still needs a nighttime bottle. He drinks well from a cup, but he still wants a bottle before bed. When will he be able to do without it?"

"I'm glad my child takes one bottle. That's the only time I'm sure how much milk he has taken. He spills quite a bit down his bib when he drinks from a cup, so I'm not sure how much he consumes."

Many children require one bottle until they are about three years old. The evening and the early-morning one are usually the last to go. Sometimes it's the child who is not ready to relinquish the bottle, and sometimes it suits the mother's needs. Parental recognition of the accomplishment of drinking from the cup may motivate a child to continue drinking from a cup.

"My child seems to be making progress in every area except sharing toys. He

still clings to his things. Shouldn't he be sharing by this time? I don't like it when people tell me he is selfish and will grow up that way if I don't do something about it."

Two-year-olds are just beginning to get the idea of thine and mine. Most are not able to fully accept sharing until they are about three years old. However, if the parents continue to indicate what is theirs and what is not, and point out that a toy is still theirs even if another child plays with it, they begin to understand the concept of sharing and taking turns.

Readiness for Nursery School

Parents are now beginning to think about nursery school and assume their children will be ready. Not all children are ready for nursery school at the same time. Differences in growth, speech, ability to cope with separation, toilet readiness, and socialization all contribute to a child's readiness for nursery school. In addition, parents need to assess early learning groups in their neighborhood to see if they are appropriate for the child. Location, hours, and necessity all need to be considered.

"I'm glad to be able to discuss nursery school, even though I know my son is not ready for it yet. In my neighborhood, many mothers become frantic about getting their two-year-olds into nursery school. You would think they were competing for admission to Harvard!"

You might be interested to know that some experts, such as Burton White of Harvard, do not think children should be in formal groups until they are three. White believes that children this age should be in a limited group—ideally, one or two other children—and only if they have no other way of socializing. At three years of age, White feels, children should attend school no more than once or twice a week. He is much more in favor of the informal kind of groups that mothers supervise.

"Mother-supervised groups worry me. My church has started groups of ten to fifteen children and two mothers. I'm concerned about these mothers' ability. Suppose your child is old enough for such a group but those in charge are not competent. Isn't it better to enter a child in a formal nursery school with trained teachers?"

We believe small groups are best—for example, three or four mothers and a similar number of children meeting for an hour two or three times a week in each other's homes or at the park. Each mother can supervise part of the activity. One can arrange the motor activities, such as running, riding together, throwing a ball, climbing, and using a slide. Another mother can supervise storytelling or singing games. Another mother can be in charge of snacks. Then the mothers can rotate their roles. This makes it more interesting for both mothers and children; it provides the opportunity to socialize and interact with other mothers and children.

"Informal groups are fine for mothers who do not work outside the home. But what about the mother who has to work away from home?"

Mothers who work outside the home have to arrange for competent substitute child care. A nursery school is not a substitute for mother, but a mother may feel more comfortable about leaving her child there than with a housekeeper who is not trained in child care.

"But a child whose mother works isn't any more ready for nursery school than the child of a mother staying home."

Readiness for nursery school depends on the child's own maturational time-table—which is a product of his own natural endowment and the effect of the environment in which he has been living. Each parent has to assess her child's development and needs and her own resources and needs, then do what is best for that child in those circumstances.

"Why are informal play groups recommended over nursery school at this age?"

Children at this age are not ready to separate from their mothers. They are just learning to interact with one or two children in mother's presence. They are not yet at a level of social and verbal development that will enable them to cope in a large group away from mother. An informal group serves as a natural transition to a larger, more formal group. The group can be disbanded when the children seem fatigued, and an individual child can be removed from the group if need be.

"When do most children appear to be ready for nursery school?"

Again, readiness for nursery school varies with each child. In general, children of about three can relate to other children, can express their needs clearly and comprehend simple directions, can separate more easily, are beginning to achieve bowel and bladder control, and have relinquished their bottles. So we suggest that a child should be considered for nursery school when he or she is three years old.

"I understand that those achievements are important, but I was wondering how often a three-year-old who has accomplished all that should be attending school."

Most three-year-olds do best when they attend nursery school twice or, at most, three times a week.

"How long should the nursery-school session be?"

In most well-run nursery schools, the session for the first weeks are for an hour to an hour and a half, and are then lengthened to two hours as the children's tolerance increases.

Separation

"Should we expect the children to separate easily from their mothers at nursery school?"

The children who are ready will separate easily. Some may even be ready to have mother leave the first day. Others need their mothers to stay for a while—sometimes for several days or for up to two or three weeks. At some schools, mothers spend the whole session with their children for the first few days, then spend the session in a hall outside the classroom or in a room provided for mothers, and then finally leave for the entire session.

"I think that when the time comes, I'm going to have a harder time leaving my son than he will have leaving me."

That does happen. Many adults carry vestiges of their own separation problems. Sometimes the mother's reluctance to part is subtly conveyed to the child. The child appears to be having difficulty separating, when in reality it is the mother's problem. Separation is a developmental issue of great significance, and it requires understanding and sensitive handling.

Teachers' Attitudes About Separation

"I understand the need to stay with a child at first, but my impression is that teachers frown on mothers' staying. What can I do if a teacher asks me to leave so that she can handle my child?"

Most nursery-school teachers today have a better understanding of this issue than in the past. Many schools have policies that allow mothers to separate gradually by standing in the back of the room, then in an adjacent room, and finally by leaving when the child appears ready to separate. This usually takes about two weeks. If the child is still unable to separate at the end of that time, the parents and teachers should recognize that he or she is not ready for nursery school.

Readiness

That doesn't mean the child has to be excluded from other types of social situations. He or she can be entered in an informal play group. Most community libraries have story hours. YMCAs offer exercise and play groups and swim classes that mothers can attend with their children.

Until about age three, children are at their best with only one or two other children. That is why some nursery schools introduce only a few children at a time to the class until the whole class is assembled.

"Suppose you are a mother working outside the home. It is impossible to spend so much time getting your child adjusted to nursery school."

Some mothers who work outside the home make arrangements with their employers and make up the time later. Other mothers have the child's caretaker stay with the child at school as long as the child needs to get adjusted.

Father's Role

"You talk about mothers staying with the child. Can't the father play a role in this too?"

■   ■

We say mother because it is usually the mother who assumes this role. Of course the father can be the one who takes the child to school and stays until the child is able to separate. It depends on the family's situation. In some families, the father's schedule is flexible enough to allow him to spend this time with the child.

"It seems that until the children are about three, we should not really be expecting them to be ready for nursery school. It's disappointing in a way because I was looking forward to doing some things on my own. But I can see that they need more time to separate, and that the time spent with them now can be very constructive."

"I'm very glad I don't have to rush to find a nursery school and that I'll have the better part of a year yet with my daughter. I enjoy being an important part of her development and having fun with her."

All parents must realize that children need time to reach the stage of development needed for nursery school, and that the time needed is different for each child. The time parents spend with a child of this age can be very important for the child's growth.

Toilet Training

In the past two years, parents have been advised that most children are not ready for toilet training. Now that the children are in their third year, parents, and sometimes grandparents, are getting more eager for toilet training to be accomplished. It is once again time to assess the children's stage of develop-ment—and parents' expectations—in this area.

"My husband and his mother are trying to pressure me into getting our son toilet trained. I'm not sure he is ready. Could we review just what a child needs to be able to cooperate for toilet training?"

First, the child needs to be able to understand that things belong in certain places—for example, that dishes belong in one cupboard, groceries in another, garbage goes in the garbage can, and toys have a shelf. The child is then able to understand that urine and stool are deposited in a special place in the bathroom.

"My child puts everything into the garbage. Would you say that is an indication he is not ready?"

Yes. He needs more time to be able to understand where things belong.

"Our son is beginning to observe in the bathroom and announce what he observes. He designates urination as 'wee wee' and a bowel movement as 'poo poo.' Does that signify that he is ready?"

He may be beginning to understand the purpose of the bathroom. He is closer to being ready for toilet training, because he is verbal enough to label a need, which is the second requirement for toilet training readiness. In addition, a child has to be aware of the sensation of a full bladder or rectum and be able to express this to a parent.

"My child is beginning to tell me—after she has soiled. That upsets me, and I've been tempted to scold her."

It's natural for parents to be disappointed at this stage. Your daughter is achieving awareness, but not in time to warn you. That awareness will come if she is reminded that soon she will be able to tell you before she soils. She is in a stage of development that will pass more quickly if she is not intimidated and frightened by parental criticism.

It is best not to make any comment that could be interpreted by the child as criticism. Parents should remember that toilet training is a big step for children. In addition to being able to recognize the need to void and tell a parent in time, children also need to be able to control their sphincter muscles until they are undressed and placed in the proper position at the toilet.

"My child has sometimes gotten to the point of telling me in time, but when she is put on the toilet seat she can't perform until she is removed and put in a clean diaper. Then she has a bowel movement in a few minutes. That is exasperating, and I'm afraid I have shown my annoyance."

In addition to being able to hold back until being placed on the toilet, children must also be able to relax the tightened spinchter in order to expel the contents of the bowel or bladder. This ability takes longer to develop. If your child has not achieved this ability yet, there is nothing to be gained by showing annoyance.

Making the child anxious may inhibit the ability to relax the sphincter. The whole process of becoming ready to have bowel and bladder control is a complicated one. Children may accomplish part of it and need more time to achieve it completely. Parents should observe and be aware but not interfere with success by trying to hurry the child.

"Does bowel control come before bladder control?"

In most cases, bowel control is achieved before bladder control, because at this age only one or two bowel movements occur during a day. However, there are some children who achieve bladder control first.

"To achieve bowel control, must a child have a regular time every day to move his bowels?"

Bowel control is more easily achieved if there is a regular time for bowel movements every day. For one thing, this allows the parents to be on the alert and available for assistance if the child needs it.

"Should I place a potty seat in the bathroom now so it will be available when my child is ready?"

■   ▪

First assess how ready your child is to control her toilet activities. If she seems ready, then it may be helpful to have the potty seat available. Some children sit on it clothed for quite a while before they are ready to use it properly.

"I put a potty seat in our bathroom a few weeks ago. It has not made the impact on my son that I hoped it would. He just pushes it around like a cart. Should I stop him when he does that?"

You son doesn't seem able to associate defecation and urination with the potty chair. To him it is a toy. It is probably best to put it away until he seems more prepared for it—perhaps for a month or two.

"Is it better to use a chair that sits on the floor, or a seat that fits the adult seat?"

Most children adapt more easily to the seat that sits on the floor. If the other type of seat is used, it should firmly attach to the adult seat. It should have back and foot rests, and a strap to keep the child from slipping out. If the seat is unsteady or uncomfortable, the child may become frightened. This may retard progress for many months.

"My child seems far from being ready for toilet training. He watches me flush the stool from his diaper down the toilet, and he gets so upset that I have to wait till he is busy playing and not watching me before I continue. Is that normal?"

Some children regard their bowel movements as part of themselves. To see part of themselves flushed down the toilet is very frightening. Until a child is able to deal with this fear verbally, it is best not to expose him to this situation unnecessarily.

"My daughter is already indicating that she wants to sit on the adult toilet. Twice she has pulled me to the toilet and, suspecting what she was trying to do, I placed her on it. She urinated once and had a bowel movement once, for which I praised her. But she has shown no interest since. I didn't know whether to suggest she use it again or wait till she tells me."

She is showing that she is developing an awareness of the use of the bathroom. When she is ready, she will let you know. There is no way to predict how soon that will be. It depends on her rate of maturation and perhaps the stimulation she gets by observing others.

"I have an older daughter. I think I tried to start toilet training long before she was ready, so I'm not going to do that with this one. However, she watches when the older one uses the bathroom; she tries to be just like her big sister. It seems to me she is going to achieve control long before her sister did."

Many children who are ready to exert control respond to seeing an older sibling or peer use the toilet properly. This is often more effective than any other stimulus—certainly more so than parental coercion.

"What about nursery schools that require that children have bowel and bladder control? Isn't that a kind of coercion?"

Not all nursery schools have this requirement. Most nursery-school administrators know that children of this age have either established control or will do so shortly. However, if parents try to force toilet training so that the child can enter nursery school, the child's progress in this area may actually be hindered.

"When my daughter has a bowel movement while she is napping, she sometimes wakes up and smears the stool all over her crib. Of course, I scream 'No, no' when I see her doing it. She seems upset, but she may repeat it in a few days. What should I do?"

At this stage of development, children like to smear. We've all noted this when they eat cereal or mashed potatoes. We tolerate this form of smearing, but we strongly disapprove of the smearing of stool. Parents can give children an outlet for smearing with playdough or finger paints, in a setting with an apron, and plastic sheets or newspapers, for example. Smearing of stool usually passes when bowel control has been achieved.

"Throughout these discussions the message has been 'easy does it.' Does that mean we should not be asking our children if they want to use the bathroom, that we should just let them tell us when they are ready?"

Children between twenty-four and thirty months are at various stages of development and ability. We have observed that when children are ready to exert bowel and bladder control, they make their desires known. The successful achievement may take just a few days of child and parent cooperation instead of a few months of struggle. Some children are successful sooner than others, but most will be successful by about age three.

Communication: Speech and Language Development

When children are between two and two and a half years old, they start to form two- and three-word sentences. Some may even form longer sentences, while a few still have not gone beyond simple phrases. Most children this age understand between a thousand and fifteen hundred words but can express only two or three hundred.

You have been anxiously awaiting the time when your children are able to talk to you. What have you been noticing about the children's speech development? Do you think they are at last acquiring the ability to express themselves?

"I have noticed a great improvement in our son's speech—three-word sentences. But sometimes I don't understand exactly what he is trying to say. I ask him to repeat it, telling him 'Mommy can't understand you,' and I feel so bad that I can't."

This happens frequently when a child first begins to talk. If you do understand what the child is saying, try saying the words clearly. He will perhaps be able to say them a little bit more clearly himself.

"We know what our daughter means. She says 'nackers' for eyeglasses and 'dazu' for diaper. I think it comes from putting together 'diaper you' and 'change you.'"

You can say, "Yes, diaper." If you say the correct word, she will catch on when she is ready. For now, the point is that she is using language.

Modeling Correct Speech

"Should a parent correct a child's mispronunciations?"

It is best not to correct them, but to simply say the word correctly. For example, if the child says "lelphant" for "elephant" you can say, "Oh, yes, that is the elephant." Don't use the child's pronunciation, but try to speak to him, converse with him, and listen to what he has to say. It's important for children to feel that they are communicating and getting responses.

"Isn't a parent supposed to correct a child's speech? If not, how does the child learn?"

The parents' role is to talk with the child and to model correct speech. For example, if the child says "psgetti" or "getti" for spaghetti, the parent should reply clearly "You want spaghetti." The child will be able to adopt this model of speaking when his central nervous system matures sufficiently.

Speech is a complicated process. Think about what it requires. The child has to be able to hear what is said, so his hearing must be intact. To say a word, he must also be able to marshal his vocal chords and the muscles for speech and respiration. Not all parts of this system mature at the same rate. And no two children develop the ability to speak at the same rate.

It is possible to understand how much variability there can be. One can also understand how frustrating it can be for both parent and child to have the parent say over and over again, for example, "say spa-ghe-tti" in trying to correct a child who is not ready to respond at that level and can only manage "psgetti" or just "getti." That is why the parent should model correct speech but not correct the child's pronunciation.

"I must confess that we are so anxious for our son to speak correctly that I have done just that—sat in front of him and made him look at my mouth as I said a word—'tri-cy-cle,' for instance."

Stuttering

Such drilling can inhibit the development of speech. The child may recognize the parent's frustration and therefore seek to avoid such encounters.

"I've noticed that my son may come up to me and repeat a syllable like 'gu, gu, go' while pushing me. I'll respond, 'Say, go,' but he'll do it again. Can children of this age stutter?"

Children of this age may hesitate or repeat a syllable. This is a result of their anxiety to communicate coupled with their immaturity. The best approach is to listen patiently to the child without offering a correction—"You want to go. I understand," for example—then matter-of-factly carry out the requested activity. In some cases this occurs when there is too much hurry and tension. The appropriate remedy is to slow down the tempo and rhythm of activity and make no comment about the speech. Given a chance, this will subside without any intervention other than slowing things down.

Bilingual Families

"What about speaking more than one language to a child? My mother lives with us, and she speaks only Spanish. My husband and I speak mostly English to each other. Should we speak only one language to the baby? Some people have told us he is slow in talking because we speak two languages in our home."

Most children brought up in a bilingual family learn to speak both languages and which to speak to whom. These children may initiate speech a little later than others, but usually no lasting difficulty results from the use of two languages. However, children whose speech development is slow—or who have a hearing impairment—should be spoken to in one language.

"My wife and I work. Our housekeeper takes care of the baby while we are working. Her native tongue is Spanish, and she speaks a broken English. We want her to speak English to our child, but she has difficulty with it and lapses into Spanish. We are satisfied, because we feel that if our housekeeper speaks Spanish and we speak English, our daughter will learn two languages."

If your child is making progress in both languages, she can only benefit from this situation.

"I work, too, and I come home late in the evening. Our son spends most of his time with our maid, who can speak both Spanish and English. But she just isn't a communicator, and she doesn't say much. Our son's language acquisition doesn't seem to be as fast as our friends' children of his age. Can this be related to the lack of speech stimulation?

Your son's timetable for speech development may be slower than that of your friends' children, or it may be that he is not spoken to enough. If a child's caretaker does not stimulate speech development, parents should attempt to make up for this lack by spending as much of their free time as possible speaking with their child.

"Can a child who isn't stimulated at home and is slow in acquiring speech make up for it when he goes to school?"

Children can compensate for lost time, but parents should bear in mind that there is a natural timetable for speech development. The best results come when we take advantage of that sensitive period when the children are most receptive to language stimulation. By this age, children should understand about twelve hundred words, understand simple commands and questions, and be able to use about three hundred words. A child needs exposure to language to achieve this level of development.

Inhibiting Communication

"Isn't it important how we talk to children, too? I have found that loud voices upset my son. If someone asks him a question in a loud voice, he cringes and can't answer."

"I remember feeling that way about one of my uncles when I was little. That tone of voice bothers me even now. So I can see how it may bother a small child."

Some parents and other adults talk to children the way they talk to adults— loudly, firmly, and emphatically. The tone of voice an adult uses may give a child the impression that the adult is angry. The child may therefore be reluctant to respond.

Another hindrance to effective communication with children is long explanations. At this age, children can't understand or process a lot of detail. They need explanations in short, declarative sentences. For instance, suppose a wheel is locked on your child's toy car. The parent may say, "Your car won't go because the rear axle has picked up a thread that wound around it. It has to be removed before it will go."

The parent could have explained more simply: "The car is stuck. Let's fix it." Then, as the car is repaired: "We unwind the thread. Then the wheel will turn and the car will go." The next time the problem occurs, the child may understand the situation and deal with it on his own.

Crying

"My child cries when spoken to firmly, and that upsets us."

Children want and need to be liked. Your son may believe that if he is spoken to sternly, he is not liked. Or he may interpret the stern words as a scolding.

"Our child cries whenever he wants something. Sometimes older children give him what he wants when he cries. We don't want him to get into the habit of making requests this way."

Children of this age are just emerging from a period in which they used crying as a language. Parents should now be patiently and gently encouraging them to be verbal and not cry for things. For example: "Tell Mommy, then Mommy can get it for you. Mommy doesn't understand what you want when you cry." Children have to be dealt with this way repeatedly before they learn that talking is more effective than crying.

Children understand instinctively that there is a change in the way parents respond to them as they get older and become more verbal. They respond well to recognition and approval in simple words they can understand. The resulting boost to their self-esteem brings on a new level of the parent-child relationship that can be most rewarding.

■   ■

2

The Importance of Play

Enjoying Playtime

Now that the children are two and older, their naps are shorter. A few children may even have given up regular naps entirely. This makes the  waking time longer and puts pressure on mother to devise ways of spending time profitability and pleasantly. Although children can play alone a little longer than before, they still demand a great deal of parental attention. How do you spend playtime with your children and how do you feel about it?

"I've noticed that my son is sleeping less during the day lately. It hasn't caused a problem—in fact, it works out well for us, because we stay outdoors longer. I take him to the park and he plays in the sandbox, or runs around with the other children. When we come home, it's time for bath and supper and then bed. He is quite ready for bed, because he has had such an active afternoon."

"We live on a street where there are many children our child's age so we just stay out and play when the weather is warm. We have an earlier bedtime, too."

"I work outside the home. Now that our son is awake more, my housekeeper has less time to do the housework. She says it is difficult to find activities to do with him. As a matter of fact, I'm not sure I would either if I were home with him all day."

Many adults do not know how to spend quality time with a toddler. This is an important period for the child. It's a time when the capacity to learn is very high and curiosity is great. But the child's increasing mobility requires parental intervention for support, for setting limits, and most important, for teaching.
Parents should remember that they are the child's primary teachers—not just guardians or, as some parents seem to view their role, policemen.

"Could you give an example of what you mean? I've always felt that children learn more in a formal nursery-school setting than they do at home."

There are many examples. One is the parents' role in teaching the words to name things, people, places, and actions. In other words, parents teach the most important tool a human being has—language. In addition, parents introduce children to abstractions. We teach children number concepts when we point out "two dogs," "three balls," or "one cookie." When we point out the "red" bus or the "yellow" truck, we teach color concepts. When we ask children to get the ball "behind" the chair or "in front of" the table or to pull the block "on" the table or "under" the table, we are teaching spatial relations. When we throw a ball "up" or "down," or to Daddy or Mommy, we teach direction.

"I never realized how significant even an ordinary daily encounter can be. I think I can pay more attention and do better at it. What about play and games?"

It is great fun to see children develop interest and understanding of games. At this age they enjoy rolling a ball to a parent or other child and having it rolled back. They may try to throw the ball but usually have little control in direction or force in throwing. They will achieve this later. They enjoy singing games like "Ring-Around-a-Rosey" and "All Around the Mulberry Bush." "Peek-a-Boo" may now advance to hiding objects under a pillow or blanket or even to "Hide-and-Seek" with child and parent. This is a very important game, because children begin to learn from it that things exist even if not visible.

"I've tried 'Peek-a-Boo' with my daughter, but she becomes frightened if she can't see me. I have to hide so she can see at least part of me. When she hides, she stands so she can be seen. Why does she do that?"

She is playing the way a child of her age plays. She is still unable to separate fully from you, and she isn't sure that you exist when she can't see you. These are concepts and experiences that she is being helped to understand by playing this game. She is not ready to play by adult rules yet; she plays in a way that makes her comfortable.

"When can children play this game as adults understand the rules?"

Children may not be comfortable having themselves, playmates, or parents fully hidden until they are seven or eight years old.

"I guess this is another example of expectations that a child this age can't meet. What other ways do you suggest for spending time with children this age?"

You can try activities that improve eye-hand coordination, like stringing large beads, lacing shoes, stacking blocks, placing simple shapes into the openings in a board or box, and doing simple puzzles. In addition, you can try large-muscle activities, like running, riding a kiddie car, climbing small steps, and sliding down a short slide. Some children enjoy crawling through a "tent" made by placing a cloth over a card table.

■   ■

Reading

It is good to follow play with quieter activities, such as looking at books and pointing out pictures. The children are beginning to be ready for books containing nursery rhymes and captioned pictures.

"Are children this age ready to be read fairy tales?"

Most children of this age are not ready for fairy tales. Learning about reality is more important—for example, understanding that one parent, or both, goes to work and comes back, and that events in their lives occur in a predictable order.

"My child likes music. We spend quite a lot of time listening to records. She likes to dance to the rhythm."

Listening to music, moving to a rhythm, and learning to sing songs are very beneficial ways to spend time. Children like to hear their parents sing the same songs over and over. It does not matter to them how well their parents' sing. Children enjoy when parents sing to them, listen to music with them, and demonstrate dancing and clapping movements for them.

"Sometimes I have to cook or straighten up the house. I can't always spend time just playing with my child, although I enjoy it. When I try to do chores, he calls to me and wants me to play in his room. I don't want to make him unhappy, so I stay with him, but I'm a little irritable and impatient."

What the child may want is to be in the same room with you. If you're working in the kitchen or laundry room, you can give a toy to the child to play with near you. If you are making a bed or dusting, your child may like to help out.

"I've tried that with my daughter and it works, but my chores take more time that way."

But you are not just getting your chores done. You are also teaching your child what is to be done, when, and how. As she learns, she gets a sense of achievement and a sense of pleasure in helping. Parents should remember that it is difficult, if not impossible, for children to hurry.

Community Resources

"I don't like to stay in the house so much with my son, but there is just so much outdoor walking and playing we can do. I get bored, and I think it's conveyed to my child. What about organized activities?"

Most communities have facilities and activities for toddlers. YMCAs offer simple gymnastic groups. Many public pools offer swimming instruction for parents and children. In some communities, there are music activities and basic arts-and-crafts groups for children. One or more of these facilities may be ideal for parents who want a change of scene and stimulation for themselves and their children.

Children can also be taken on short exploratory trips—such as to the post office, grocery store, or local fire station. Most children enjoy zoos, especially petting areas reserved for young children. Many museums have special activities for young children and their parents. Trips to a store should be for specific items; children this age shouldn't be expected to tolerate long shopping trips.

"I like to visit friends who have children close to my child's age. But these visits often have to be cut short because the children can't get along with each other. Then I feel cheated out of visiting with my friend and am a little cross with my child. Are children of this age too young still for visiting?"

Children of this age, between two and three years, can manage and even enjoy visiting, but they do best with only one other child. They still need adult supervision and cannot be expected to negotiate sharing toys without supervision. Their visiting behavior improves as they become more familiar with the host child or children, and the host parents' attitudes. The visiting child should bring one or two toys of his own in case the host child has difficulty sharing. It is important for the parent to recognize that the priority is to help the child learn to socialize, not for the adults to socialize. As children become more experienced with interactive play, they may be able to play for as long as a half an hour with a parent nearby.

"When can children be expected to play together without needing parents to settle squabbles?"

That varies with each child's ability to socialize and the socializing situations provided. Most children older than three are able to play together reasonably well, and get increasingly better from then on. However, there still may be instances in which parental intervention is needed, even with school-age children.

"It is nice to hear how other mothers spend time with children. It makes me feel that it's possible to be with a child and not be bored, and at the same time help her develop."

Spending time with children has gotten poor press from people who do not fully understand the parental role. Many parents who understand that their role is to teach creatively and be supportive get a great deal of satisfaction out of watching the children develop.

Toys

Toys are important to children. Parents should keep in mind that the attachment a child has for a certain toy may be an important part of the child's emotional development. Loss of a dearly loved toy can cause a

■   ■

child a great deal of needless anguish, and can interfere with the separation process.

Many parents are concerned about the quantity and quality of toys they make available to their children. Have any of you been thinking about this issue?

"My concern is having too many toys around. When I notice that my child hasn't been playing with certain toys, I put them away. If he later wants anything back, I pull it out again."

It is good that you don't give away, or throw away the toys, as many mothers do. These toys may be ones the child has become attached to and from which the child has gotten a sense of security. A child whose toy is thrown away may feel as though she has lost a friend. It's much better to save the toys in a box and bring them out again as they are needed. When a toy is reintroduced, the child can be shown a way to play with it more imaginatively.

"When I was a child, the toys were made of wood and didn't wear out easily. My mother still has some of them."

"My husband still has an old stuffed elephant that he had when he was a child, but he can't understand our child's attachment to certain toys."

Adults sometimes forget the attachments to toys they had when they were children. Recalling these attachments may enable parents to be more in tune with their children.

"We have a big toy box in which our son settles down and plays. Sometimes he digs deep and pulls out old toys. They are never put away for long."

Many parents store some less-used toys away so that their children have something stimulating when other toys lose their attractiveness or novelty.

Mother's Capacity to Play

"My son is often cranky when he is confined to the house. I didn't realize that he may be tired of his old toys and need something new. I thought it was because I was inept at playing with him."

Mothers differ in their capacity to play with their children. However, every child has a need to relate to the parent through play. So it is important to notice the kind of toys your child enjoys. It's also important to enhance play by introducing different toys and activities periodically as the child's interests and comprehension increase. Between two and two and a half years of age, children enjoy toys that require them to insert simple shapes into appropriate spaces, although some children may need a little assistance at first. Many mothers make this kind of toy from a milk carton or plastic jar by cutting shapes of cardboard to fit the holes of the same shape in the containers. The shapes may be brightly colored with vegetable dyes.

■ ■

"I've done that, and it works well. My daughter sits on the floor and keeps herself busy with this activity for half an hour or more."

That is a long time for a child to concentrate. Another activity that children now enjoy is putting objects into a wagon or shoe box with a long string, then carting the objects from one part of the room or house to another. This often becomes a delivery-man game later on.

Children this age also like simple puzzles of two or three pieces and one with handles on the pieces. They also like to stack measuring cups and try to arrange the cups in size order, although some may not achieve this until three years of age.

"I gave my son a few small cardboard boxes of different sizes to play with, and he cherishes them more than store-bought toys. He works at fitting the boxes into each other. Some days it keeps him busy for almost an hour! But some days he gets frustrated and throws the boxes away. Should I give him something else to do then, or show him how he can do it?"

First assess how upset the child is. If his frustration is great, he may not respond to your efforts to help. If that happens, try removing the toy and introducing another activity. If there is less frustration, show the child how to overcome his difficulty. It is important to do this as unobtrusively as possible so that the child doesn't feel you are taking over. If the toy continues to frustrate the child, possibly he is not ready for it. It would be best to retire the toy for a month or two.

"I was wondering if big beads strung on a shoelace are all right to introduce now."

Strung wooden beads that can't be swallowed—about one and a half to two inches in diameter—are appropriate for a child of this age. Sometimes these beads can be purchased with a lacing frame; an old shoe can serve the same purpose.

Parental Supervision

All of these activities enhance the child's eye-hand coordination and manual dexterity. Many children also enjoy pasting and coloring now.

"I'm afraid to start my child on activities that involve pasting or coloring. We'll have it all over the house."

Pasting and coloring should be done under parental supervision, in a suitable place and manner. These activities should be reserved for times when a parent can give undivided attention. If the child pastes or colors in any place other than the one designated for it, the activity should be discontinued.

"I guess I've been doing the wrong thing. I tell my child to color only on the paper, but when I look again she has been coloring on the chairs, the walls, everywhere. I get angry and scold her."

Children of this age still need constant supervision when involved in activities that can end destructively.

Security in Repetition

"We have been spending a great deal of time indoors looking at books. However, my child sometimes wants to read the same book over and over again. When I try to introduce a different book, he protests. Is that normal?"

Children may enjoy a familiar book many times in succession. It helps them verify what they know and gives them a sense of security. Some children will explore a new book on their own and finally ask to look at it with a parent.

"My child just wants to roll a ball or his cars back and forth. He never seems to tire of it. How can I introduce something else?"

Some children have to be allowed to expand their interests on their own timetable. However, a parent or caretaker can introduce something that accommodates the child's interests, such as building a tunnel, road, or train tracks with blocks. This may arouse interest and start the child on other activities.

"Our baby wants to hear the same record over and over again. He has a few nursery rhymes and lullaby records. He can tell by the cover which is the one he wants. He can pick it out of a pile even if I try to conceal it."

Children do become attached to certain songs and rhymes just as they do to toys. However, many children listen to other music when played on the adult cassette player and may increase their repertoire that way. In addition, there are records with action directions and games that are fun and satisfy a child's need to move around as well.

"My child doesn't have a cassette player, but we sing a lot together and clap and march to music. We enjoy it, and I find visiting children enjoy it too."

Sounds

From time immemorial, singing has been part of growing up. Singing is a very good way to relate to a child through music. Children of this age also like musical toys such as drums and xylophones.

"Someone gave my son a drum, but we had to take it away because we couldn't stand the banging."

The banging gives him a sense of achievement and power. But if the drum is too noisy for you, the tops of the drumsticks can be covered with sponge. This mutes the sound but allows the child to enjoy the toy and the sound it produces.

"I made a drum for our child with an empty oatmeal box and two ice cream sticks with sponge at the tips. That rescued a rainy day for us."

"This gives me an idea of what to do with the hammer of our daughter's pegboard. I'll paste sponge on the tip so the noise won't bother me so

much. *Also, there may be less chance of her getting hurt when she misses the peg."*

These are ways to allow a child the freedom to bang, which is one of the activities she may enjoy for the feeling of power it gives and the satisfaction she receives from coordinating hand and eye movements.

Attachment to Toys

"My child's favorite toy is a Raggedy Ann doll. She repeats with her doll most of the things I do with her. She changes her, feeds her a bottle, pushes her in her stroller. The doll is a mess. She has other dolls in better shape, but she wants only this one. I've been tempted to replace it with a new one."

It's best to let your daughter keep the doll. The appearance of the doll may be just what endears the doll to her. Even an exact replica will not be the same for her.

"My son has an old, ratty stuffed dog that he is so attached to we can't go anywhere without it. When do children give up old toys?"

Aside from the attachment a child develops for an object, the object may represent to the child a link to parents. That is, the toy may become a transitional object, which helps a child make the transition from total dependence to independence. So these toys must be treated with care and respect in the child's presence. All of children's play should be treated with respect because it is children's "work." The importance of children's play and toys is just beginning to get the attention it should.

The Effects of Television

There is ongoing discussion and controversy about the effects of television on children. Which programs should they watch, at what age, and for how long? Does violence on the television screen stimulate violence in children? Is television too stimulating before bedtime? Does prolonged television watching affect children's creativity? What does it do to a child's ability to relate to people? What ideas do they get about life from television? Are they confusing reality with fantasy?

The children are older now and more apt to be exposed to television. What are your feelings about the effects of television, and how much television do you let your child watch?

"I guess I use TV to quiet my child down. When he gets overexcited, I put him on the sofa and turn on the TV. He gets so absorbed that he simmers down almost immediately. Then I can put him down for his nap."

"My experience has been just the opposite. My daughter is often scared by things on TV, especially some announcers in commercials. She comes running to me while pointing to the screen and saying, 'Man! Man!' "

"I find I have to use the TV as a baby-sitter—sometimes because I don't have anyone else to watch my daughter when I'm doing something that I need to concentrate on, such as preparing a meal, making an important phone call, or even going to the bathroom in privacy."

We're not concerned about instances when the television is used for a limited time, but rather when it is used for hours on end while a parent or caretaker attends to other matters. This is not at all an uncommon practice.

"What harm is there in allowing the child to watch television if she is quiet and content, and it allows the mother some time to complete some of her work?"

A child left in front of a TV set is being deprived of the parent's company. The child is also deprived of learning experiences that he or she gets by observing and participating in what the parent does—for example, making a bed, cooking, putting things away. Any such activity is a learning opportunity for a child and provides a chance for communication that the TV does not.

Violence

"I've always worried about the violence that children see on TV. Even children's programs have violent episodes sometimes. What effect does TV violence have on them?"

Many studies have been and are now being done on this issue. While they are inconclusive, some studies show that violence seen on TV can evoke violence in easily aroused individuals. Certainly the vast amount of violence seen on TV can desensitize a child and make violence seem a normal way of life. The consequences of that attitude are frightening to comtemplate.

"I've noticed a difference between the games played by children who watch TV and those played by my child, who hasn't watched TV. We don't have a TV set so my child has not been exposed to any of the things you mention, but he is being initiated by others. When I hear this going on, I step in and suggest some other game. It doesn't always work, but I try."

Children who watch TV a great deal are so influenced by it that it cuts down on their originality and creativity. Some children act out violent scenes or relate to fantasy situations. Others are attracted to lavish displays of cars, clothes, food, and musical styles that are presented on television.

"I understand what you mean. Children who watch a lot of TV are deprived of the normal spontaneous play that they need and are exposed to situations and concepts that shouldn't be part of their lives. So they don't really have a normal childhood."

■   ■

"I understand that too and it worries me, but what can I do? I set the TV to an appropriate children's program or a nature program and go out of the room for a minute and when I come back there is something violent being shown. You just can't avoid it."

"That happens to me too. When I realize that the program is different, I turn the set off. Then my son begins to cry and complain. I try to distract him and get him interested in something else, which usually works. But I don't know what he has seen while I was away and whether it was harmful or not."

"I try to get an idea about a program before turning it off so I can figure out what may cause anxiety or confusion for my child. Then I can talk to her about it."

It is good to try to find out the child's interpretation of what she is watching so that you know her level of thinking and have a clearer sense of what to explain. This approach is better than simply correcting the impression you think the child may have received. Ideally, parents should watch TV with their child so they know what the child has been exposed to and can better help the child deal with her interpretation of a program. This is not possible if the child watches TV alone.

"Since TV can be such a confusing experience, isn't it best to not have any TV at all?"

Some parents have used that approach, and it can work with small children. But as children get older, parents cannot always control their TV viewing. TV is apparently here to stay. There *are* some worthwhile educational programs. The sensible approach is to allow your child to view only those programs that meet with your approval. Children learn to accept this just as they do other events in their lives that are arranged for them.

"In our house, we turn the TV on only at news time. My son usually is in the living room with my husband at the time. Some of the news is pretty terrifying even for me. Should we remove our son from the room, even though he doesn't want to leave Daddy?"

There is another solution. For example, Daddy can watch the news later at night and read or play with your son when he first gets home. If this is not possible and your son is in the room with Daddy when the news is on, he may not always be watching anyway. Remember, children of this age do not have a long attention span. However, your husband should be aware of when and what your child is watching. He can find out how the child interprets what is being shown on TV, then explain and clarify as necessary.

"I think the TV has cut off communication in many families. We may sit glued to the set and not exchange a word for an entire evening. I think TV should be monitored for parents, too."

■   ■

Judicious use of the TV would help many families, parents, and children alike. Perhaps we could get back to talking more to one another or reading more. Certainly, many children love to be read to. In addition, reading to a child helps to ensure success in school later on.

Learning to Play with Others

There is now beginning to be more interactive play. As the children socialize more, sharing of toys becomes a pressing issue. Many parents expect children to share toys readily, and the child may be reluctant—in fact, may vigorously protest the suggestion to share. Parents must realize that sharing requires a maturity that a child may not yet have achieved. Children are usually better able to handle sharing at the playground, which is everyone's turf, than at home. In addition, a child recognizes which children play in the manner he enjoys and shuns the ones who don't. Have sharing and play with other children become issues for any of you?

"There's always a sharing problem when another mother visits with a child my child's age. Shouldn't my child be able to share toys by now?"

Children between two and two and a half are just beginning to understand what is theirs and what is not. They do not emerge from the "I, my, mine" stage until they are about three. The ease with which children learn to share is also related to the experiences they have had. For example, if a child has been forced to give up a cherished toy before he is ready to do it, he may be reluctant to share other toys.

"Maybe I've been expecting too much. I've been making my son give his toys to visiting children. I know my friends expect me to see to it that my child shares with their children. If I don't do that, won't he grow up to be selfish?"

Parental Fear of Selfishness

Many parents worry that their children will grow up to be selfish adults. However, a child this age who refuses to share is not being selfish in the sense that adults understand the term. The child is only trying to establish his identity, part of this involves claiming what belongs to him.

"But it is so embarrassing when he refuses to share. What can be done to ease the situation?"

First, understand the level of your child's development in the area of sharing. Then tell your guest beforehand what behavior is characteristic of him. Until children are comfortable with each other, they may play only with their own toys. Perhaps you can suggest that visitors bring one or two of their own toys so that an exchange can be made.

"A friend from out of town came to visit with her little girl, who is my daughter's age. My child was holding her doll when we went to the door.

■   ■

The other little girl reached for the doll, and mine drew back and said, 'No!' in a very emphatic, unfriendly tone. My friend was carrying her daughter's favorite Snoopy, so I said, 'Yes, the dolly is yours, but see what a nice Snoopy she has.' As soon as her coat was off, my friend's daughter followed my child into her bedroom, holding her Snoopy, and in no time at all, they warmed up to each other. I can see what unpleasantness there could have been if I had insisted that my child give up her doll to the visitor."

"When other little boys come to play with mine, it seems they all want the same thing—the tricycle. My son will push another child right off the tricycle if he wants it."

Perhaps you can say "It's his turn" and hold on to him, then turn to another child and say, "Now it's your turn." If you do it for each child often enough, they will get the idea that each boy gets a chance at it. This is the beginning of learning to take turns.

"If I did that with my child, he would be kicking and screaming."

Yes, but if you do not get upset with him and instead help him have his turn and keep repeating the turns, he will begin to wait his turn because he will understand that he will get a chance. Try to arrange the turns so that they come quickly and often.

"I can arrange these situations better on the playground than at home. Why is that?"

It may be that because it is not his turf, your son can accept taking turns better. At home the toys are his possessions, so he can't give them up as easily. Parents should remember that when another child takes a toy, the host child may think it has been taken for good.

"I keep telling him that his toys are not going to be taken away, that they are his. I say, 'You will keep the toy. A friend is just visiting you. When we have a friend visiting, you let him play with your toys for a little while and you play with his. When you visit him, he will let you play with his toys, too.'"

Simple Directions

Maybe that's too long an explanation. Instead, you can say, for example, "This is yours. Adam will play with it now, and you will play with Adam's toys." Friendship may be too sophisticated a concept.

"Is it too sophisticated to say, 'When you are at Derek's house you play with Derek's tricycle, and when Derek is at your house he can ride your tricycle'?"

Try to offer a direction—not an explanation—and say it in as few words as possible. That's what children understand best at this age.

■   ■

"I have noticed that my son can't share certain toys no matter what toy the other child has. That makes for a difficult situation, especially when we invite someone for the first time."

If you can anticipate the situation, it is certainly wise to tell the other child's parents and suggest that he bring a toy or two of his own. It is also a good idea to put away your child's favorite toys and leave out only the ones that are easy for your child to share. Of course, that does not guarantee that all will run smoothly. Sharing is a difficult concept for children to learn. Parents have to assess how ready their child is for it and not attempt to force the issue.

Parents can model sharing by offering the child something of their own. For example, suppose the parent is eating or drinking something that the child wants. The parent can say, "I will share my sandwich with you." Then the parent can reverse the procedure and ask for something of the child's. Through repetition of such episodes, the child gradually develops a less threatening view of sharing.

"My child doesn't want to play at all with some children, let alone share a toy. It's very upsetting if the mother of the other child is a good friend. Should I make him play with other children?"

Children's Choice of Friends

He may have had a previous unpleasant experience with the other child. Even at this age, children can tell which children play with them in a way they enjoy and which do not. But they may not be verbal enough yet to explain this preference to you.

"I think I know what bothers my son. This other child, who is in our play group, is a very active, vigorous child. When he wants something, he pushes to get it. He is a nice child—not mean, just aggressive. My son gets very upset if he is pushed. He doesn't like to be touched, let alone pushed."

"My daughter is like that. She never grabs something she likes from someone else, but she's always having things grabbed from her. She keeps away from children who do that."

"We have a similar problem. My son has two friends who are just like him, but another one is very aggressive. He pushes, bites, fights, and intimidates. My son is terrified of this boy. He'll say, "I hope he's not coming today, and I don't want to go to his house."

That other boy must have done something that your son didn't like. You shouldn't leave your son in the play group when that boy is there or when it's at that boy's house. That will only intensify his feelings about the other child, and he may develop a fear of being left in any group or at any child's house.

"We have a neighbor whose child will be two next month. This child and my daughter play constantly and share nicely."

■   ■

The gentle children are sometimes the ones who have the problems in groups. The rough, aggressive ones seem to get along better.

"My son is quite active, and he is shunned by many of the other children and their mothers. There are very few houses that we can visit. When we do visit, I have to be involved with the children every minute."

As a rule, very active children get along better with other children who are active. These are children whose interest is directed toward large-muscle motor activity. These children should be given appropriate outlets as much as possible. In the suburbs or country, there is room for them to run and chase. In the city, these children can be entered in an activity group that encourages jumping, running, and climbing. These children may then be able to settle down to quieter activity when that is called for.

"I'm glad to hear that there is nothing wrong with active, assertive children. My son is one of the active ones—'motor oriented,' I've been told. My best friend's little girl is afraid of him, and because of that we don't see each other and it has caused a rift in our relationship."

This does not have to be a permanent situation. You can continue your friendship and socialize at night when the children are asleep. As the children grow older and mature, they may be able to get along on a verbal level and even enjoy playing together. As children get older, there is growth and change in all areas—social, physical, and intellectual.

"I'm glad to hear that this sharing problem is just a stage, and that they will later be able to cope with children they steer clear of now. But how long does that take?"

As we have said, much depends on the child's maturational timetable and how much she is exposed to different situations. In most cases, it takes a few months.

Playing Alone

As children grow older, parents may become anxious for them to play more by themselves. Children do begin to play alone now, but usually not as long as parents would like. Children of this age are just beginning fantasy play. Some may even have imaginary playmates. While this amuses some parents, others become concerned. Have you been seeing any change in the children's play routines recently?

"I've noticed recently that my son will play alone on the living-room floor if I'm there too. He doesn't seem to be aware of me at all until I go out of the room. Then he follows me."

"The best time with my child is in the kitchen. When I'm cooking, I give him pots and pans. He strews them all over the floor and can enjoy himself and

■   ■

let me work for at least fifteen to twenty minutes. Sometimes he has me taste what he is making, but mostly he just talks to himself."

The children are more able to play alone in your presence. Some can take on roles—driving a car or cooking, for example—that encourage them to play alone for a limited time.

"My daughter is interested only in her doll. She doesn't make any effort to play with anything else. She feeds, changes, dresses, and undresses it. She diapers it with facial tissue—loads of it—then takes it for a walk in the doll stroller. Sometimes she sounds as though she is scolding the doll. I get the impression that she is imitating me."

She is assuming the maternal role, trying to better understand the world around her. Many children imitate their parents, and this gives parents the opportunity to see themselves as their children see them. That can be beneficial for parents; it may help them improve their parenting methods.

Fantasy Play

"My daughter is always taking my pocketbook or my shopping bag. She puts it over her arm and pretends to go shopping. She even goes out of the room and comes back with an item or two—a doll or one of her books, for example. She is particularly interested in having a set of keys so she can open the door to come back from the store. She is clearly imitating what we do almost every day."

She seems to be fantasizing that she is the mother. That makes it possible to separate from you, to go down the hall alone and away from you. Children are now reaching a stage of imaginative play that helps them sort out their experiences. Parents should make an effort to observe a child's play during this stage. It gives a great deal of insight into children's level of development and the way they interpret events in their lives.

Parental Intrusion

"I've been doing that. Believe me, it's an eye opener! I was wondering if parents should just watch or get involved. Once in a while I try to get into the act, but my son will say 'No' and wave me away. I guess I'm a little hurt."

This feeling of rejection is understandable. Now that they have more imagination, children like to feel they can at least control their own play, and they regard parental participation as an intrusion. A more realistic and positive way to regard this attitude on the part of the child is as an advance in development.

"I guess I've been anticipating the time when my son could play more alone. It seems to have come suddenly and taken me unawares, so I felt rebuffed. Looking at it the way you just put it makes me feel better."

"Do you mean that we should never get involved when they are playing alone from now on?"

A better approach is simply to notice what the child is doing and recognize it—"Oh, you are putting your doll to bed," for example—but not make a gesture to assist if you're not invited to. Children may regard such a gesture as intrusion. At this stage, most children like to have what they are doing recognized and labeled.

Transitions

"What if you have to go someplace or dinner is ready and you have to interrupt playtime? When I do that there is usually a scene, with much screaming and crying."

Children this age have difficulty making transitions from one activity to another. Suppose you have to go out to an appointment. The child can be warned several minutes in advance. After that interval, you can say, "Now, it's time to go." If the child still resists, quietly but firmly tell her that she can finish whatever she is doing when you return home but that now you are going to go out. Name places of interest on the way and what the child will do when she gets there. That is, give her a scenario of what is to come so that she doesn't feel the end of her playtime means the end of all play. If you use this approach consistently, she will get to know that you mean business and that there is a procedure you follow.

Imaginary Friends

"My child plays alone pretty well for her age and can change activities fairly easily—with one exception. She has an imaginary friend who goes everywhere with us. I don't know whether to be upset and try to discourage her, or to go along with her."

"My son has just begun to have an imaginary dog. At first we thought it was amusing, but he is so serious about it that we are getting a little worried."

"My child has many imaginary friends, but they all have the same name—whether it's a teddy bear or a doll or another little girl—so it's sometimes hard to figure out which one she means."

It is not unusual for a child to have imaginary friends. At this stage of development, children can't fully distinguish between animate and inanimate—the real and the fanciful. They endow everything with the same abilities that they themselves have. For example, it may seem to a child that a doll should talk. The child convinces herself that the doll does talk, and the doll becomes a real companion.

"My daughter gets so busy with her doll, feeding her and tending to her. When I call for her lunch she brings the doll too, and insists it sit with her at the table. One spoonful of food is for her, the next for the doll. Of course,

this procedure slows down our meals. I don't know whether to go along or show my annoyance."

Children who play alone a good deal are more apt to resort to imaginary playmates. They so want someone to play with that they may invest an available toy with the qualities of the friend they want to have. You should recognize this and say something like "I know you'd like to have a friend to play with, so you are making believe Teddy is your friend and you want him to come to your tea party." Then, you can join in the fantasy.

Children need fantasies. It is the parents' job to help them distinguish what is real from what is fantasy without derogating the fantasy. Fantasy is related to creativity, so it should be dealt with thoughtfully and sensitively.

"I guess we just assumed that children understand things the way adults do and accept what is real and the way we see it. I must confess I was a little surprised and annoyed when my son wouldn't let his grandfather sit down in a certain chair because that's where the imaginary friend, the toy dog, was sitting. I insisted he let Grandpa sit there. Grandpa just laughed, but I made a scene and my son cried. From now on I'll do better, because I understand what's going on. How long does this stage last?"

This, too, varies with each child and family situation. In some cases it lasts the better part of a year; in others it remains intense for a much shorter time. It usually disappears as language and means of testing reality becomes a little more advanced. The important thing is not to be angry, show alarm, or make fun of the child.

■   ■

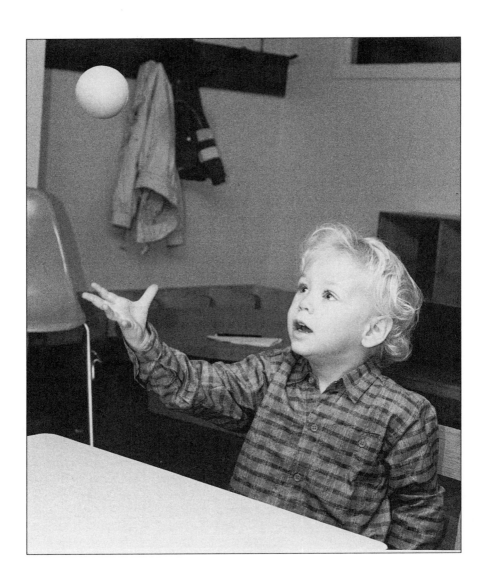

3

Understanding Your Child's Personality

Your Child as an Individual

Parents are beginning to recognize the personality characteristics of their children. Some are pleased with the way the child's personality is developing.  Others may find that the child is developing differently than they had hoped or anticipated. Some parents worry that they are trying to mold the child into a replica of themselves; others are actually trying to do this. At one time, infants were thought to be born with a "clean slate" and had no inborn abilities. We know now that infants are born with a specific endowment and a certain capacity for developing that endowment. How well that endowment flourishes is affected by the environment the child encounters.

What have you been noticing about your child's development as a person? Do you think of your child as a person with his own special personality, or as a replica of you or someone else in your family?

"I've thought a lot about our child's personality. He appears anxious in some situations, such as visiting in an unfamiliar house. I keep wondering if he is going to be an anxious person all his life. He never takes the first step to make friends."

"My daughter makes friends with everyone at once. In fact, she seems to take over every situation she is in. Of course, that is cute now, but will that quality make her unpopular when she grows up? I guess I worry because my sister is like that. We never got along, and I'd hate to have my child be like that."

"Our child is so different from both of us. We are both very quiet and reserved. He is so outgoing and boisterous that we have said jokingly that there might have been a switch of babies in the hospital."

We have all seen children who are aggressive, who bound into the room and take in everything in sight and participate immediately. Other children come into a room and simply stand and watch. Likewise, there are some grown-ups who are mixers and back-slappers, and there are others who are friendly in a quiet way. Some like a lot of noise and turmoil, and others like to stay away from that. So it is with our children—each personality is unique.

"I have to laugh sometimes, because our son seems to be getting so much like his father. He resembles him physically. He seems to be getting his hearty laugh, and he seems to have the same walk. I like that, and I know my husband is thrilled when anyone says, 'He's the spittin' image of you.'"

Some parents feel uncomfortable with a child whose personality is different from their own, and want their children to resemble themselves as much as possible.

Parents' Upbringing

"I have a different attitude. There are things that are part of me that I don't want our boy to have. I don't want him to be so inhibited that he can't express his feelings without a great deal of struggle and the help of therapy."

It is natural for parents to want to avoid what they interpret as mistakes in their own upbringing. Are there particular issues you have in mind?

"I want to try to avoid being as critical and demanding as my parents were of me. If I got ninety-five on an exam, for example, they would say, 'You should have gotten one hundred.' So, when my little girl plays with a toy and she doesn't get it quite right, I try not to say, 'That's not right, push this a little bit this way,' because I'm trying to build self-esteem. In that way, I guess I am trying to influence her personality."

Your recognition of her accomplishments is an appropriate way to influence her development and enhance her self-esteem.

"I had a big hang-up about food and separation. My two things were that my son should never have separation anxiety and should never be fat. So far, the food issue has worked out very well. But when I see him cling to me so much, I get worried. I think that I may not be handling this issue correctly."

Apparently, the separation anxiety you experienced has made you more sensitive to it. It may appear to you that your son clings to you more than necessary because of this sensitivity. Most children this age have not yet accomplished separation and may not do so for some time. Try to evaluate behavior in light of what is age appropriate.

"I want love and encouragement to be present in my home. Now that I'm older, I understand that this was lacking in my mother's home. Also, I want my child to be more aggressive than I was. I was nervous, shy, and stuttered as a child and I want to spare him that. Therefore, I am ultrasensitive when he gets upset, and I try to comfort him. I feel that the emotional aspect of child rearing is very important."

"My daughter is just like her grandmother, or at least I think that when she is very determined. That's good, although if she were more like me she would be easier to get along with."

■   ■

Natural Endowment Versus Parental Influence

"How can you tell what is natural endowment and what is parental influence?"

Some of a child's behavior is modeling after the parent, and some of it is endowment. If the parent hollers, the child will holler; if the parent slaps, the child will slap; if the parent is gentle, the child will be gentle too. There are also patterns in families from generation to generation that seem to indicate a certain genetic endowment—an inclination to athletics, the arts, or the sciences, for example. Even then, we cannot be sure how much is the result of modeling and how much is the result of genetic endowment.

"My child is developing a very irritating personality. He still wants everything, when he wants it. I say, 'Wait a minute' and he bursts into a tantrum. If that's his personality, then I want to influence it. But how?"

Children don't like to be constantly put off. You don't always say "Wait a minute" to your husband because he wouldn't like it. So you can imagine how being told to wait can affect someone whose frustration tolerance is short. A child is simply not able to wait as long as an adult.

Setting up a battle line when the child is trying for autonomy (the normal age range is eighteen months to two and a half years) establishes a pattern of relating with other people that the child may carry into adult life—a tendency to throw tantrums or to anger easily, for example. This goes on into adult life, so that social contacts have an angry quality and often end in disappointment.

This is a very crucial period; it demands of parents a great deal of patience and understanding of the child's personality.

"My child always wants to be involved in what I am doing. If I allow that, all goes well."

The way to deal with this situation is to involve the child. That makes for a more comfortable, happy atmosphere at home. But it takes a lot of time. There has to be a "fit" between mother and child's personality, and the person who can do the adapting isn't the child. Many parents were brought up to think it was the child who had to conform. The outcome of this approach has been adults who cannot manage in life or who are terribly angry every step of the way.

Parents' first job is to form the groundwork for basic trust by being available for children's needs. Now parents are dealing with character building and social responses, how children are going to relate to other people as they grow up. It is important to do it right. Looked at that way, child rearing becomes interesting and exciting and not tedious.

"Is the way we assess children the way they turn out to be? Do our preconceptions influence them?"

■   ■

Parental preconceptions do influence children, but the children's endowment will not permit you to mold them in certain ways. They themselves are just now telling you that; this is why this period is so hard. For example, some children rush into a situation and do things immediately, while others stand back and assess the situation. Again, we cannot change these tendencies—they are the result of endowment. What can be influenced is their environment. For example, setting up a parent-child relationship in which everything is a battle leads to a problem-filled pattern of relating with other people. What we are trying to establish are ways of coping with natural endowment. We are not trying to make a retiring person a hail-fellow-well-met, nor a hail-fellow-well-met a retiring person, but rather to recognize fundamental differences and respect them.

Violence

"What about violent behavior from boys and its effect on their personalities later?"

"I took my son to a three-year-old's group yesterday and the mothers said to me, 'Just wait and see, all boys get locked into climbing. He's going to be Batman and Superman and he's going to want guns.' That made me think. Are these violent tendencies really inevitable?"

Research has confirmed that boys tend to be more aggressive in their play than girls. But that does not mean that boys are more violent. The violence comes from imitation. A child who has a tendency to be a little more active can be stimulated to be more violent by television, by violence at home or on the street, and by things that are read to him.

Children's play is an indication of how they believe life should be led, or of how it appears to them to be led. If children witness violence, they may internalize it as an acceptable way of life. It is the parents' role to point out nonviolent alternatives. This is a very important area of parent-child interaction.

Fears and Anxieties

Parents are sometimes surprised and worried when their children develop new fears. In an attempt to allay these fears, many parents make light of them by saying something like "That's silly. There is nothing to be afraid of." Or they may insist, for example, that a dog "won't hurt you," then have the child pat the dog, only increasing the child's fears. If a child is afraid of the dark and claims there are monsters, a parent may turn on the light, look around, and say, "See, there are no monsters. Now go to sleep." To the parent's surprise, the child becomes even more frightened when the light is off again. It may help to ask what the child thinks the monster will do and to agree that it frightens him and then leave a small light on in the room on, so the monster won't reappear.

■   ■

Now that the children are getting older and doing more, have you noticed that sometimes they surprise you by suddenly becoming afraid of certain situations?

"My son loves the zoo. But when we get to the monkey area, he immediately says 'Go now.' He's not scared of small animals like the raccoons and birds, but he is clearly afraid of large animals. Once we had a little girl with us who was the same age as our son, and she wasn't afraid of anything."

Two children of the same age in the same situation may not react in the same way. Your son was frightened. The little girl was not. How did you feel about that, and what did you do to help him?

"To tell the truth, I was a little dismayed to find him frightened when the little girl was not. I said, 'You don't have to be scared. Mommy and Daddy will protect you from the animals,' but he wasn't comforted until we left to go to the birdhouse."

Parental Response

When children are frightened, it is important to let them know that you understand their feelings, that you are not critical of them, and that you will protect them. When they were smaller, it was sufficient to pick them up and hold them close. Now that they are older, the best thing is to walk away from the frightening scene as quickly as possible to something that is nonthreatening.

"Later, at home, when I began to tell his grandparents about it, he was upset and put his hand over my mouth to stop me. So I guess he felt that he should not have acted that way."

He must have picked up some cues that made him unhappy to have the incident reported. It's better not to talk to others about a child's fears in the child's presence.

Time to Work Through Fears

"How can you get a child over this feeling? Do you just let it pass and say nothing about it?"

One of the ways you can handle this situation is by recognizing the fears and avoiding those situations that make the child fearful until the child has had a chance to work through his fear in play. If he is afraid of large animals, he can look at pictures or toy replicas of the animals, talk about the animals with you, and imitate the sounds they make. Sometimes children play the role of the animals themselves and, in that way, discover that they are not threatening. The child can perhaps be told about another child who had the same fear and overcame it.

"I thought I could just tell my son not be afraid and he'd accept that."

That's what many parents think, and that's why they become impatient with their children. Children need time to work through fearful situations in their own way and at their own pace.

"We bought our daughter a toy mouse in a cage. She wouldn't come near it for days. Then it hit us that she was afraid it would get out. When we told her the mouse couldn't get out of the cage, she was able to play with it and enjoy it."

It is important to allow children to tell you what they are thinking. Parents get used to talking to their children about their own feelings, but neglect to take time to understand the children's interpretation of events and circumstances.

Need for Consistency

"That happened with us last Halloween. Our daughter was terrified of a mask her father put on."

Some children become fearful when their parents wear clothes different from those they usually wear. They certainly can't tolerate masquerade costumes on their parents. Many parents are disappointed at Christmas when father puts on a Santa Claus suit and the child becomes fearful and cries. Children have a fixed image of what father and mother are like; dressing in a way counter to that image may shock a child and undermine his or her sense of security. Most children of this age do not take to new situations readily.

Darkness and Other Fears

"My child has recently become afraid of the dark. What could have caused the change?"

There are many explanations. Sometimes a child is awakened by a loud noise, can't distinguish the objects in his room, and becomes frightened. Or a gas pain may awaken him, and subsequently he associates the pain with darkness and becomes upset if put to sleep again in a dark room. Sometimes this fear develops after a difficulty in a play situation with another child. Or a disturbing dream may awaken the child, and the unpleasantness of the dream becomes associated with the dark. To understand the cause of a fear, a parent has to be aware of the child's experiences.

"My child insists on having the light on at night."

A night-light usually helps a child overcome fear of the dark.

"My son insists on having the whole room lit up. He goes to sleep only if I leave the overhead light on."

It is a good idea to ask why he needs it on. A dimmer can be attached to the light switch. This allows you to lower the light little by little until your child is comfortable with less light.

■   ■

"I think my child is upset by anything that makes a loud noise. The vacuum cleaner, the electric mixer, and even the toaster upset him. When I use any of these appliances, I have to put him several rooms away and close the door. Then he gets upset because I'm separated from him."

He may learn to cope with the appliances if he is allowed to inspect and play with them when not in use. He may imitate the sounds of the appliances and then be able to tolerate them when they are being used. If there are toy replicas available, play with them may help, too. However, overcoming anxiety over separation from you is not so easily accomplished. Fear of separation—from mother particularly—is a very important issue. It is best, therefore, not to intensify this fear by separating from him while he's trying to cope with a more easily resolved fear.

"Our son has recently begun to fear going down the slide in the park. He used to love it, and we can't understand why he is now afraid of it."

It is possible that he is now aware of how high the slide is. So his fear may indicate an advance in his understanding.

"I think that explains why my daughter suddenly no longer likes to swing high on the park swings. She is just content to sit there and sway back and forth a little. As far as we know, she was never pushed off or swung so high that she was frightened."

"Certain tapes upset our daughter. For example, when we come to parts of Hansel and Gretel, she covers her ears and runs away till the dance part comes on. So we decided not to play tapes like that anymore."

"My son is afraid of a certain man in TV ads. Whenever he comes on, I simply turn the TV to another channel. I don't understand why this man upsets him."

Many things may frighten children of this age. The child is immature, inexperienced, and unable to explain why certain things bother him. Parents should convey to the child that they understand his fears and that they are there to protect and help him. It may take a long time before the child can verbalize the reason for these fears.

Separation

The process of separation and individuation is understood by researchers and students in the field of child development, but parents may not realize how long it takes for a child to separate comfortably from them. The child may cry, refuse to play or be consoled, or become quiet, sad, or angry. This may even happen when the parent tries to move the child from one activity to a new one, or put the child to bed. What separation issues are you encountering now, and how do you handle them?

Child's Response to Separation

"We are still having difficulty with this, usually when our daughter is over tired and my husband and I go off in the car. She feels that she should go

too, and she cries at the door and throws herself on the floor. It is so upsetting to us."

Your daughter can't understand why she can't go with you. Knowing that this is the way she reacts when overtired, you may be able to anticipate and avoid it to some extent. It may also be helpful to point out to her that, just as in the course of her day there are times when she goes out and comes back, so also mommies and daddies must sometimes go out and come back—emphasizing the coming back. Also, let her know what she can be doing when you are away. She may still protest, but the misery is usually somewhat diminished.

"Our son, too, becomes extremely upset when we go out together."

Children of this age still may become very anxious when their parents leave them, even when they are left with someone they know and like. When children first begin to walk, they move away from mother without realizing what they are doing. They may be so pleased with their new accomplishment that they don't immediately notice the temporary separation. When they realize they are away from mother, they run back to her. If parents try to push children away at this age, they may cling even more. If mother is in the kitchen, an area may have to be set aside from which the child can see her. Similarly, many children have difficulty starting nursery school. For most children, separation is not accomplished until around three years of age.

Early Day Care

Early day care can be a difficult time for children because they are being made to separate before they are ready. There is less of a problem over separation if the mother understands this and gives her child undivided attention for a while when the day-care session is over.

"It is more difficult for a child to be left in a different environment? Is it different from leaving the child with a baby-sitter in your own home?"

Leaving the child with a familiar baby-sitter in the child's home is the best arrangement. Another solution is to leave the child at a neighbor's house that is familiar. Familiar surroundings and routines make separation less upsetting for a child.

Separating Gradually

"I have an opportunity to put my son in a play group with four other children. At first I will be staying with him, but eventually I want to leave him the two hours of the session. I am worried that he may not be ready."

At this stage your child may be ready to spend time in a new setting—as long as you are there too. Perhaps when he becomes more secure there you can try leaving for ten minutes, then half an hour, then for the entire session.

"What is the danger in not 'weaning' a child gradually from mother?"

If the child is forced to separate prematurely—before she is ready to cope with it—separation anxiety may set in. The effects of separation anxiety can interfere with her ability to cope throughout her lifetime. For example, some young married adults live in the same apartment house with, or next door to, one set of parents. Sometimes we refer to this as a close-knit family, but it may instead be the consequence of an inability to separate. We often hear of children away at college who get extremely homesick. That, too, may be related to separation anxiety.

Some children are able to separate at two and a half, some not until three and a half or even later. It is different for each child.

"We are beginning to have a better appreciation of the effects of separation issues. When we came back from California our daughter never wanted her daddy out of her sight, and she wanted us both to bathe her. We thought it was strange, but now we understand."

We all know that a child has to learn how to sit up, crawl, and stand before he or she can walk. But some parents do not understand that separation is a process as well. Some get stuck in the middle longer than others, some make it through very rapidly, and some need longer for the final transition. Every child achieves separation on his or her own time schedule.

"Our son has not been sleeping since we came back from Florida about two weeks ago. Shouldn't he have gotten over our being away?"

He apparently needs more experience with your being home. He may have missed you most when he was put to bed.

"Well, to tell the truth we left at night when he was asleep, so he may be afraid we will leave again when he is asleep."

Your child needs assurance that you will stay. It may help to tell him that you and Daddy are home now and that you are going to stay. Perhaps if he realizes that you understand his worry he will feel more comfortable and be able to sleep. Parents sometimes prolong the effects of traumatic events through their inability to understand what is troubling the child.

"My son has been very upset because his daddy has been away, but he is talking about it, saying, 'I want Daddy to come back.' He says it even when he knows Daddy is at work during the day."

He is probably saying it because he needs reassurance.

"He got a big reaction from me when his father went away, and I complained over the phone to my husband about his being away, telling him how much our son missed him."

■   ■

Your being upset only made it harder for your son. Children easily pick up the mood of parents. It can signify to them that something is indeed wrong—in this case, that perhaps Daddy is away forever.

In addition, when Daddy now leaves to go to work for the day, the child is worried that Daddy will stay away. It's important to tell him that Daddy will be home in a little while. He is at work and will be home before the child goes to bed.

It is a good idea to have children visit a parent's place of work so they can picture where the parent goes after leaving home. This may make the parent's daily departure less frightening.

Nighttime Separation

"Our child puts up a fuss even when we are going out to a friend's, to dinner, or to a movie. He's usually all right a few minutes later. Can we expect him to understand an explanation like 'You're a big boy now. Mommy and Daddy are going out and we will be back soon, so don't cry'?"

It is normal for children of this age to protest. But the protest need not be protracted. A competent baby-sitter can engage the child in some pleasant activity. Repeated experience with parents' leaving and returning will enable the child to cope eventually.

"Our daughter cries hardest when we put her to bed. She clings and seems afraid to be left alone. We tried leaving a light on in her room, but nothing seems to work except sitting with her until she falls asleep."

Many children find bedtime separation the most difficult, especially if it interrupts play with parents. Children need a simmering-down period and a fixed routine each night that leads to bedtime. Some children may still need parent's presence until falling asleep.

"My child used to have a difficult time separating at bedtime. Now she puts her dolls to bed first and tells them to go to sleep. Then, when we tell her it is her bedtime, she seems to accept it."

Parents can help a child with bedtime separation. For example, the child can be told a story about another child who spends the day as your child does, then goes to bed and, on waking in the morning, finds Daddy and Mommy have been sleeping in their bed and are happy and healthy and ready to get up.

"When I leave my son at Grandma's or a friend's, he protests but then quickly gets involved in some activity. But when I come back to get him, he puts up an even louder protest because he doesn't want to be taken away from whatever he is doing. He seems glad to see me, but he doesn't want to leave. It seems he has a problem separating from everything."

Many children have difficulty making a transition from one situation to another. It is hard for them to separate from friends and pleasant situations, or to separate at bedtime if they are in the midst of pleasant play with Daddy and Mommy. It sometimes helps to let them know what they will be doing next, such as going home for lunch or to play with their dolls or to meet Daddy. In that way, it doesn't seem like an ending but a beginning of something else.

There are more aspects to separation. We have discussed some of them here, but this is an issue that will continue to come up.

Sexual Identification and Curiosity

Most parents find it difficult to deal with children's curiosity about sex, gender and sexual identification, and nudity. Many parents are very anxious to learn how to deal with these issues and have many questions. They want to know how much a child needs to know and what to say to satisfy their curiosity.

"My son has been aware of his body for quite a few months, but now it seems he is noticing more than just his anatomy. It seems he is noticing the difference in sex. When do children begin to do that?"

At around eighteen months, children become aware of—and start naming—their body parts. You probably have seen that recently. Now, when they are between two and three, they are becoming aware of their genital organs and of the difference between the sexes.

Naming Body Parts

"My son ran into the bathroom when my husband was bathing, looked his father over, and then pointed to his genitals, saying, 'That, that.' I guess wanting to know the name. My husband said, 'That's Daddy's penis.' Our son said 'Peen?' and ran out of the bathroom. My husband wasn't sure he had done the right thing."

The first time that happens, no matter how intellectually prepared we are to respond appropriately, parents may be taken by surprise and fumble for the right reply. When children point to genital organs, parents should name this part of the anatomy just as they would name the knee, eye, or any other part of the anatomy. We don't want children to feel that genitals have some special significance.

"Should children be given the proper anatomical names or special names? My sister's children refer to their private parts as 'wee wees.' Of course, they will have to learn the real names later in life. I want my child to learn and use the proper name at the start. Is that okay?"

It is now considered better to give the proper anatomical name. You can tell your child that a male organ is a penis. The female has a vulva, which

■ ■

is an external part of her anatomy, and a vagina, which is an internal part. However, often the female genitalia is simply referred to as the vagina. The child can also be told that the female also has breasts.

"When do children begin to know what sex they are?"

They are beginning now to recognize themselves as boys and girls. With most children, gender identity is firmly established by three years of age.

Nudity

"In order for children to observe the difference between male and female anatomies, they have to see their parents nude. I've talked to several mothers about that and there seems to be quite a difference of opinion about it. In some primitive tribes, everyone goes around nude. Is that harmful?"

It depends upon the customs of the people and what is accepted in their culture. In ours, we tend not to expose our bodies.

To little children, the standing adult may seem very large and threatening. Consider the view a small child has when he stands next to a nude parent. His eye level is at about the level of the parents' genitals. For some children such a view may be too stimulating; for others it may be upsetting. They may want their private parts to be the same size. They may question why they do not have pubic hair. Girls often question why their breasts are not as large as mother's. Size is very important to children; they view many situations in terms of size. Since we are not certain at what age and how a child will react, it is best to limit unnecessary exposure to nudity.

"What if my child comes in when I am taking a shower or about to get dressed? What should I do?"

Finish the shower quickly and cover up in a robe or towel without making a fuss. If you are undressed, get into your clothes quickly and casually. If you draw too much attention to the situation, the child can be given a sense that there is something wrong with the human body and, by association, something wrong with his own body. Of course, we don't want to foster this impression.

"My husband and I did not pay much attention to our daughter's presence when we were dressing until she was about eighteen months old and began to point to parts of our bodies. We named the parts for her—breast, penis, and so on. I told my mother, and she had a fit. She said our daughter was too young and that we'd make a sex maniac of her."

"My parents reacted the same way. As a result, we began to feel uncomfortable, so we were careful to be dressed or covered when our child was around. But shouldn't children be learning the difference between the sexes about now?"

The children are getting to the stage when they do have to know the difference between the sexes. But they shouldn't be threatened by differences in the anatomy, or be overstimulated by it. Responding to children's questions about sex frankly and naturally is the best approach parents can take.

Noticing Sexual Differences

"What about seeing other children nude?"

That should be treated in the same way as adult nudity. If a child sees another child of the opposite sex undressed and is curious, anatomical parts—including genitals—should be named matter-of-factly.

"That situation came up a few weeks ago. My best friend, her husband, and their son came to spend a weekend. When we undressed the children to put them to bed, we gave them baths. My daughter watched the boy, a few months younger than she is, in the tub and she was very curious about his penis and lifted her nightie and looked at herself. We said, 'That is his penis. He is a boy. This is your vulva. You are a girl.' She seemed to accept that explanation. Was that right?"

That is exactly how a parent should respond in such a situation. Children come to accept sexual differences when they are presented honestly and matter-of-factly.

"Should children be allowed to play with each other in the nude—say, for an afternoon?"

That is not a good idea, because children compare their bodies. For some, differences in size may cause concern. Girls may worry that they don't have a penis. Some children may be stimulated to do more touching of themselves or others than is appropriate, and this may arouse sensations with which they are not able to cope.

"But we don't want them to develop hang-ups about their genitals."

Nor do we want them to be sexually stimulated before they are emotionally prepared for it. Many adolescents today become sexually active much too early, and it may be partly due to too early exposure to sexual situations. On the other hand, we don't want children to become prudish or afraid of sex. It's not an easy issue to handle, and it's not something that can be decided for every child in the same way.

The important thing is for a boy to be aware that he is a boy and for a girl to be aware that she is a girl, *and* that it's very good for a boy to be a boy, and very good for a girl to be a girl, so that they get the sense that each one is good in his or her own way.

"But I thought the idea was that it shouldn't be that boys do only this and girls do only that?"

There will always be a difference in anatomy, sexual capacity, and sex roles. That is all that this early lesson—boys are boys and girls are girls—is suggesting.

■   ■

Of course, we should not limit the experience of girls just because they are girls or that of boys just because they are boys.

It's good for boys to play with dolls because they are getting a sense of taking care of babies. It encourages a sense of gentleness. Similarly, girls should play baseball. Sports and games encourage girls to gain a sense of sturdiness and physical competence. We want each sex to have access to all the opportunities that help make them complete people.

"Most of my friends have girls. Does it matter that my son plays mostly with girls his age?"

Children should be encouraged to play with other children of both sexes, and parents should try to arrange such situations.

"What could happen if a boy played only with girls?"

The boy may experience pleasure in playing with girls and their doll play to the exclusion of other experiences. He may think it's much nicer to play with girls because girls have everything, since he doesn't have the experience of having the things and doing things that boys do. Such situations, while unusual, are not a cause of concern now because children are just establishing their gender identity and parents can arrange to have appropriate play situations for both sexes. The opposite situation can operate in a similar fashion for a girl exposed only to boys. She may then prefer only boys' activities. So it is important for boys and girls to have playmates of both sexes.

"I sometimes see my son rubbing his genitals. Why does he do that?"

Some children do a lot of touching of their genital area. It may be simply an act of discovery and exploration. But if it is done to excess, there may be another reason. For example, the child may have an irritation or clothing may be rough or too small. For some children, such touching is comforting. Others simply need to know that they are still intact.

Masturbation

"When does masturbation start?"

Some children start very early. It is typical of children who are left alone a great deal, or who are put into their cribs for a long time alone. Children who are kept busy and stimulated masturbate much less. It often occurs that when children first discover their genitals, they need to touch them frequently. Some then begin to get a sensation of pleasure and use that to comfort themselves and masturbate. When they have other interests, that need disappears.

"How old do you think children should be before they are told the facts of life? A lot of people think the earlier, the better. But this seems wrong to me."

■   ■

It all depends on the child and his or her experiences. At three, children are naturally curious and should be given explanations, but only on the same level as the questions they ask. Don't go into the details of reproduction if all the child wants to know is the name of the hospital he or she was born in.

"Won't some explanations scare a child this age?"

No explanation should be made in a way that frightens a child. It should be only as sophisticated as the question—and the child—seem to warrant.

Children interpret everything concretely. If they want an elaboration, they will ask for one.

"I think you are taking their childhood away somewhat when you tell them too much. But my friend says, 'It's a new world now.'"

It *is* possible to provide too much sexual information too early. It is best to ask what the child thinks is the answer to his question, then the answer can be on the child's level of understanding, and in direct response to what the child is asking. Right now, most children are asking only about the differences between boys and girls and trying to establish their own sexual identity.

■   ■

Discipline: A Teaching Process

4

Setting Limits

Agreement and consistency between parents is very important in establishing discipline. Now that the children are becoming more verbal, a new level of understanding and relating is required. To set discipline priorities, there has to be agreement between parents on what activities are to be limited. If one parent sets certain limits and the other sets different ones, the child may become confused and overburdened.  This situation may be further complicated by a housekeeper or grandparents with entirely different ideas about discipline. Are you having any difficulty agreeing with each other on the setting of limits?

Parental Disagreements

"Setting limits is the one area where we have the most disagreement. I think my wife is overprotective. I understand that some things are dangerous, and I agree they should be limited, but I want my son to be like a boy."

"I understand my husband's fear that I'm undermining our son's masculinity, but he's not with him all the time. For example, I don't allow our son to climb on the sofa, because he can tumble off if I'm not in the room to watch him. But his father allows him to climb, because he is sitting right there."

Every child needs to exercise and to learn how to climb. However, your child can't distinguish yet that climbing on the sofa is all right when Daddy is there but not when he is home with Mommy. Perhaps you can let him do his climbing in a park that has climbing equipment, or in your yard if there is a place to climb. This way, both parents can permit climbing under supervision and limit it at home.

"I won't let our daughter walk in the street unless I hold her hand. My husband lets her because he says he can catch her in time."

Right now, the goal is to have the children accept the limits set by parents as they learn to exercise control themselves. It is dangerous to experiment with a child's judgment on a busy, overcrowded street. If the child cannot accept holding a parent's hand, she should be confined to her carriage until you reach a park or other safe area where she can be allowed to walk alone.

"Last week, we got into a rowboat with our daughter. Halfway through the ride the child wanted her life jacket off, so I let her, despite my wife's protests. Then our daughter leaned over the edge and nearly fell out. This taught me a lesson. A parent can't always predict what a child this age will do, so it's better to be prepared. I now understand my wife's attitude."

Of course, each parent has the child's best interests at heart. The important issue is to know the child's level of development, then give her clear messages and set consistent limits. When parents reinforce each other, a child accepts limits more easily and feels more secure as well.

"I know when our son is going to do something that he should not, so I warn him beforehand. My mother thinks I should let him do it first, then say 'No.' "

You are right to anticipate and help him not do it, so that you don't have to say 'No' to him afterward. Suppose, for example, that he likes to pick up a certain ashtray. If you see him going toward it, you can give him something else to pick up or distract him in some way. This way, you don't encourage him to do something that you have been trying to teach him not to do. Many parents wait to see if a child has achieved control instead of helping him to achieve it by anticipating the prohibited activity and offering an acceptable substitute. This way is harder—it takes patience and time—but it is most effective. The other way expects control by the child before he has the inner control that comes from appropriate disciplining.

Threats

"I'm trying to anticipate, but it is not working. When we are going out and I know my son doesn't want to put on his snowpants, I'll say, 'If you don't put on your snowpants, you can't go with Mommy.' We still have a scene, and I have to force him into the snowpants."

That is anticipating, but you are threatening him as well. Threats may evoke fear and oppositional behavior in children.

When the child is busy playing and the time comes to go out, give a warning such as "Pretty soon we will be going out to the park to play. When we do, we have to put on our coats and snowpants." A little later announce that it is time to get ready and proceed with the dressing. The child may protest less, because he has not been threatened.

Protests

"But what should I do if he still protests?"

You can quietly continue dressing him while telling him about all the things he will see and experience when he goes out. The child will begin to accept that snowpants go on before he goes out, and the protests will diminish. It takes patience and persistence on the parent's part, because this is a learning process that takes time.

"When I take my daughter to another child's house to play, she doesn't want to leave when it's time to come home. So I say, 'If you don't want to come home, I'll go home and leave you here.' She cries and protests, but she still doesn't want to come home. So I take her home crying most of the way."

If this becomes a pattern—always threatening but never carrying out the threat—you will lose credibility with her. In addition, such threats may frighten the child and thereby interfere with the trust relationship between parent and child. Instead, tell the child that it will soon be time to go home and that you will leave as soon as the activity is finished. This gives a warning, while letting the child know what to expect next.

Bribes and Bargaining

"I use a different method. I say, 'If you come home with me I'll give you some cookies.' Or we'll stop for a hamburger or something. It usually works."

"I sometimes resort to that approach too. I do it especially if I want him to stop playing and come shopping with me, which he doesn't like. I say, 'If you come shopping, I'll buy some cookies for you.' "

The way it is stated—"If you do this, I will . . ." makes it a bribe to induce the child to do something. Instead, try mentioning an activity or object you know interests your child: "When we go home we can stop on the way to look at the fire engine" or "When we go to the market you can help push the cart" or "When you stop crying we can go for a ride." This way, you construct a sequence of events, a scenario the child can follow, and you won't be trapped into giving bigger and better bribes.

Remorse and Apologies

"I know that a good relationship between parent and child is important. Sometimes I do explode when my child has done something wrong, like throwing her food on the freshly scrubbed kitchen floor. Then I apologize and say, 'Mommy didn't mean to holler but you made me angry.' I don't know if she understands, but I feel better."

"Sometimes I lose control too, and then I'm full of remorse and I apologize."

This can confuse the child. If the child's behavior is not acceptable, she had to know that you disapprove. But if she understands that you are apologizing, she may not understand that you are apologizing for overreacting. She may think you are apologizing for disapproving of what she did. It is best not to apologize until your child can understand this distinction.

"Do I do irreparable damage if once in a while I explode?"

Parents are human too. We can't be in control all the time. Sometimes children try our patience beyond our tolerance. Sometimes there are combinations of stresses and the child's behavior is just the last straw. The important thing is that explosive anger should not be the standard way of expressing disapproval. An occasional angry outburst will not do irreparable damage to a child's psyche.

Discipline Versus Punishment

Setting limits consistently is an important part of parenting. The manner in which this is done is especially important to some parents who experienced harsh disciplining in their own upbringing. Some may feel that it is the only proper way to bring up children. Others go overboard to avoid this method, and may become too lenient or inconsistent. Other parents confuse discipline with punishment, or measure their success as parents by the way their children "mind" them. Do any of you find yourself in these categories?

"I was brought up by parents who were very strict and didn't believe in 'sparing the rod and spoiling the child.' So I guess I do measure my parenting that way."

"I know my parents watch how we bring up our son and how we discipline him. They think we should punish him if he is naughty—a slap on the hand if he touches something he shouldn't, for example. Should we be beginning to punish him?"

You are equating discipline and punishment. Many people use the words interchangeably. Even some dictionaries offer "discipline" as a synonym for "punishment." But there is a difference between discipline and punishment. Discipline is teaching right and wrong—what is acceptable and what is not—by setting firm and consistent limits. Punishment is teaching limits by inflicting pain and by conditioning a child to behave a certain way through the threat of pain, not through a recognition of what is appropriate behavior and what is not.

"Is punishment just physical?"

There is mental or emotional punishment, too. For example, leaving a child home because he is naughty or not giving him something he wants may inflict mental but not physical pain.

"What if I say, 'You have to put on your coat or we won't go out'?"

■   ■

That's a threat of mental punishment.

"Then how do I let my child know what will happen if he doesn't put on his coat?"

You can say, "When you put on your coat we will go out." That is a simple statement of a sequence of events. "If you don't put on your coat, I'll spank you" is a threat of physical punishment. "If you don't put on your coat, I'll go without you" is a threat of mental punishment.

"What's the harm of punishment?"

That depends on the severity and frequency of the punishment, and the child's endowment. Some children respond by becoming inhibited and unable to show any initiative. Others become angry and lash out at everyone who tries to limit them. Other children become very ingratiating. An angry child can become an adult who can't accept authority in school or on the job and goes about life with a chip on his shoulder.

Self-discipline

"I believe in self-discipline. I want our child to achieve self-discipline."

Self-discipline results when a child has had consistent limit setting for unacceptable activities and recognition for acceptable activities.

"How far along are our children in achieving this?"

That brings us back to what we have called the life history of "No." When the children were infants and began to explore things that were dangerous, we said "No," removed them from the object, and gave them something else to explore. Then, when they were beginning to move about and got into things, we said "No" firmly, and the children stopped just long enough for us to reach them.

Then they reached the stage—and some of our children are still in this stage—when they look back to see if the parent or caretaker will help to keep them from doing the prohibited activity. Some parents say the children are teasing—that they know the activity is not allowed. That's true. The children are looking for the parent's reinforcement because they do not yet have sufficient self-control. Some children are now getting beyond this stage. They approach an object, look at it, and say "No, no" to themselves but still touch it. In the next stage they will approach the object, say "No," and move off to another activity on their own. That indicates the achievement of self-discipline.

"When do they achieve this?"

That differs with each child, but most children who receive patient and consistent discipline achieve self-discipline at about the age of three.

Parental Self-control

"That means we have a while to go yet. It takes so much patience, which I don't always have. Some days I find I'm saying 'No' constantly."

Sometimes parents are upset by other things and take out their frustration on the child. The child may be going through a period of transition in which he seems to be doing everything wrong. Parents have to recognize those periods and respond to them appropriately. If the parents are patient and understanding, this stage will pass. As we have said before, limitations should be as few as possible and consistent. The emphasis should be on reinforcement of acceptable behavior.

"As children, both my husband and I were constantly scolded and punished. We both agree that we don't want to repeat that pattern. But how do we let our child know what behavior we don't approve of?"

You should be consistent in telling your child what you won't permit and what you will. For example, your child should know that you are displeased or angry with her for drawing on the furniture with lipstick. But she should also know that you approve of her drawing with a red crayon on paper supplied for that purpose.

"That method worked for my son for the stove and electrical outlets, but now he has taken to running away from me on the street."

"My son doesn't put his fingers in light sockets anymore. Instead he tries to connect the appliances with the sockets or unscrew light bulbs and reinsert them. So I have to stop him, but he balks and gets upset."

"At the beach, my daughter constantly runs into the water without waiting for me. She loves to have the waves splash over her, but it's not safe and I can't let her do it."

As children get older they want to explore and try new activities. If these activities are not safe, parents should not allow them, no matter how great a fuss the child makes. For example, if the child will not hold her parent's hand while crossing the street, she should be picked up and carried or put into her carriage. Similarly, a child who runs into the water at a pool or beach should be made to wear a safety device and be taught to wait for the parent to accompany her. Going in the water alone should be allowed neither at the seashore nor at a pool. Children who connect or disconnect electrical appliances need to be taught that this is not allowed; take the appliance or cord away and give the child something else to connect— such as pop beads or toy train tracks. In these cases, parents can't expect children to understand the danger, or to have the judgment to perceive it. Parents teach safety by setting consistent limits. Now that the children are more verbal, they can be told certain things in advance. Parents should use simple statements that the children can understand. For example: "We are going to the park. When we walk to the park we hold Mommy's hand all the way. Children who don't hold Mommy's hand go in the stroller."

"I'm always afraid my daughter will become as inhibited as I was. Isn't that a danger when a parent is too firm?"

The danger lies not in being firm but in being harsh and too restrictive. Of course, practices like running into the street, leaning out of a car window, and playing with matches should be limited firmly. But severely limiting less dangerous activities—like banging a toy, riding a scooter around the house, leaving a toy on the floor—may inhibit a child or lead to a very difficult relationship between parent and child. It may also lead to unsatisfactory personality development.

"If I explode sometimes, do I set back everything I've accomplished?"

Parents have their moments, too. They may be tired or having difficulty coping, and may "explode" just the way the child sometimes does. But if this is an infrequent event, the effects are not lasting. However, it may be harmful if it becomes the usual manner of relating to a child.

Expressing Disapproval

Many parents admonish children by issuing sharply worded commands. This method usually does not result in compliance, and sometimes the children respond angrily themselves. How readily do you expect your children to comply with a request or command?

"I expect my child to come when I call him. He understands what I want, but usually he doesn't come. That makes me angry sometimes."

"My child always picks the time I'm busiest—getting dinner ready or getting ready to go out—to get into some mischievous activity. When I call to her to stop, she usually doesn't listen. And if she does listen, she sometimes gets into something else."

Parents sometimes expect children to listen to their commands, even those issued from across a room. This is an ineffective measure for children of this age. They usually respond only when the parent is physically close.

"Do you mean if I'm standing at the door ready to go out and my child is dawdling with a toy, and I say, 'Come, we're going out now,' I should go and get him."

It will save time and energy, and avoid frustration if you warn your child of the next activity, and then take your child's hand and say firmly "It's time for [whatever the activity is]. You can take your toy with you." Or "We'll see your toy when we come back. We are going to . . ." and you recite all the interesting things the child will be experiencing in the next activity.

"I find my difficulty is when I'm busy with something I can't leave, such as mixing something on the stove or sewing curtains on the machine, so I feel I scream and yell a lot. He doesn't listen and that is exasperating."

Children this age get very involved in their own activities and explorations. They can't understand that these activities may be dangerous or annoying to adults, so they don't respond. They are not being purposely disobedient, although it may seem that way to parents. If the parent knows she is going to be busy, she should get the child involved with an activity near her.

"I thought that since my daughter understands what I want I could save myself the trouble of stopping what I'm doing and just tell her."

She is still too young to respond to that approach. If a parent is consistent with limitations and approval, the child will in time be able to internalize the limitations and then limit herself—usually beginning *after* age three, although a few children begin sooner.

"I have noticed that the louder I yell to my child, the less response I get. If I use a firm voice and really mean what I say, I get a better response."

Many parents feel that the child's response will be in proportion to the volume of the request. But children respond better to firmness than loudness.

"You have to mean business, don't you? You can't be halfhearted about it."

The parent has to be sure of herself, know what she wants, and convey it to the child by facial expression, tone of voice, and body gesture. Sometimes a parent says something in a stern voice but with a bit of a smile. The child doesn't know whether to respond to the smile, which signifies approval, or to the voice, which signifies disapproval.

"I'm afraid I do that, because I don't want to seem too harsh. My parents were very stern, and I can still remember how frightened I was when they told me to do something. I guess I'm trying not to do that to my child."

"When my child doesn't respond, I get very angry and yell. I have noticed that my husband looks stern, says his say firmly, and gets a much quicker response. Now I understand why. I must have been confusing my child."

It is important to say what you mean and mean what you say. Children feel more secure when the message is clear.

"Some children get very angry when they are interrupted. For example, when I stop my child from banging a toy against a table and direct him away from it, he gets angry and tries to knock something over. His angry response bothers me."

"My son often bites or tries to bite if he is stopped from doing something. Then there are two things to stop. I don't know which is better, to let him go on or stop him and then have him bite!"

Children don't like to be stopped in the midst of doing something, so they may protest. Biting is a primitive expression of anger. Your child may be able to understand a firm "We don't bite people. Apples and crackers are for biting. Tell mother you don't want to stop. Then we'll see what you can do instead." When this becomes your procedure—to be firm and explicit—this type of behavior gradually lessens.

"I come prepared with something to bite and I can anticipate it and ward it off and he bites very rarely now."

Parents have to expect protests, because children do not yet understand restrictions and causality—for example, "If you bang on a glass table, it can break." "If you don't come now, we'll miss the bus."

In addition, parental restrictions interfere with a child's need to establish autonomy and independence. So parents have to anticipate these protests by issuing a warning and then carrying out the accepted activity.

"What bothers me is that there are so many things that have to be limited. I feel as though I am saying 'No' all day long."

It is important to make the limits as few as possible. If we are constantly limiting our children, they get to view the parent as only limiting. It is equally, if not more, important for parents to offer approval when that is appropriate, so that the child doesn't develop a negative view of her relationship with her parents.

Recognition Versus Praise

"But I can't go around all day praising everything my child does."

We are not talking about praise, but about recognition for routine activities. Comments such as "You finished your cereal," "You opened the door by yourself," "You held on to the railing," and "You made a picture" all acknowledge little things that children do that parents may notice but don't usually recognize overtly. You don't have to say "How marvelous that you did this," but simply offer positive recognition conveyed by a pleasant tone of voice and expression.

Coping with Advice from Others

When grandparents and relatives come to visit, they are often critical instead of helpful. Part of the difficulty comes from the conflict between old and new or different beliefs about child rearing. Some grandparents feel that their children are spoiling the baby. Others are overanxious about safety matters and tend to inhibit the children's activity and development. Still others let grandchildren do things that parents don't allow.

Many older parents try to deny their grown children's independent status and need to continue to exert some control. Often they do not have time to see the new parents in action. They come for short visits and the young couple wants to impress their parents with their competence in child rearing. The young parents regress and become anxious as they look again for parental approval . . . or try to avoid parental disapproval. This leads to a very uncomfortable situation that is frustrating for both generations. Do you find your parenting methods are very different from your parents' and friends' methods?

"I have trouble, not only with my relatives but sometimes with my husband, because he is so influenced by them. They all think I'm spoiling the baby when I respond to his cries."

New ways of child rearing are often threatening and upsetting to people who have reared children themselves. If you get angry at the advice and just seethe inwardly when your relatives don't view things your way, you don't accomplish much and may hurt your relationships. It may help to say something like "I respect your point of view; I know you've had a lot of experience. Let me try to explain why I am doing it a little differently. I think this way is working out. If it is not successful, then I may try your way."

"My family says, 'You and your special methods! You think your child is something special.' I tell them that he is something special, and I remind them that they must have felt the same way about their children."

"It's very hard for me to speak out like that. I have an aunt who has three grown children, and all are in psychotherapy. Recently, she scolded me unmercifully for letting my little girl hug me. I felt like saying to her, 'Well, if you did more of that with your children, they wouldn't be where they are today.' "

It is easier to keep quiet. You might be able to handle your aunt by saying "You know, Auntie, everybody has their own way of bringing up their children. You brought up your children your way, the best you knew, and I am trying to bring up my child the best way I know."

"It is easy when we are talking about it here, but when she is literally screaming at me, I go to pieces. My husband just laughs."

Your behavior to her revives your whole childhood experience. She's still doing just what she did to her own children and you. It is very hard to escape from your childhood role when it is forced on you. That is one of the reasons why we talk so much about helping our children establish self-awareness early. If they develop self-confidence, they will be better able to cope in such situations.

■   ■

"I have the same problem with my in-laws. They do it with their older son, but they are beginning to do it less with me. Maybe I'm beginning to feel more secure and maybe it's because my parents are not that way."

"I get the same thing. There is hardly a time that I go to the grocery store that somebody doesn't say something of the same kind to me."

"The other day a lady said to me, 'That doesn't seem to be a very good toy.' The baby was busy chewing my keys and enjoying herself. It was keeping her quiet and contented while I was doing my shopping. I simply said, 'I think she will be all right.' "

"My father has the same ability to put me in a state of panic."

Yes, and then it's hard for you to remember that you are a grown-up. You are an adult; and you are really on a par with him now. You are a parent. He has a great deal of interest in you, he has a right to have an opinion and to express it, but he really has no right to direct you. It is perfectly all right to listen to him and then say, "Yes, I see you would have liked that better."

"It is so easy to say it here, but so difficult to do at home."

After a while, you will learn to make use of what seems helpful. It is like a music lesson. It seems so easy when your teacher explains it. The hard part is to go home and use what you learned. But practice makes it easier each time.

"I have trouble with my older brother. My son often wants to be carried after we've walked a short distance outside. Sometimes he is tired, and sometimes I think the traffic frightens him, so I pick him up. My brother says, 'Put him down. Do you want him to be a mama's boy?' I get upset. What makes me so insecure?"

That is not a sign of insecurity as a mother. You know what to do as a mother and you know what you expect of your child. You are not reacting to your brother as your child's mother, but rather as his little sister. He is putting you back in the mold of little sister, and not allowing you to emerge into your role as mother.

"I have had similar problems, although I think I am getting more confidence in myself. But sometimes the old feelings seep through when I'm with older members of the family."

That is not surprising. Look at how many years you were under your family's influence and how short your experience as a mother is. Mothering isn't as familiar a role yet. Your family is probably having a hard time seeing you as a mother. They don't allow you to assert yourself as a mother, and they bring back old insecurities. You have to teach them that you are becoming secure in your role as a mother.

■   ■

Conflicts also arise over different attitudes toward child rearing. We spoke earlier of spoiling. Are there other areas that cause disagreement?

Induced Anxiety

"I'm in trouble with my mother most of the time now that the baby is getting around on her own, especially if the baby tries to climb up into a chair or run down the hall. My mother is always saying, 'Be careful.' "

"I have a similar problem. How can you cope with a grandmother who is extremely nervous about everything the child does? If she sees him start to walk, she says 'Pick him up; he is going to fall' and she makes us all nervous."

The overanxiety can influence the child's development. This is another instance in which the parent has to stand up for the child's freedom to explore. It is not easy, but the parent has to patiently assure the anxious relative that the child is capable. You can stand close to the child and show the grandmother how well the child does and overtly recognize the child's achievement. Say that you know children do fall and that you watch to see that the child does not injure himself.

"I try to do that with an aunt who just dotes on the baby, but I find myself getting angry at her. She acts as though I am not aware or don't care—that only she has the baby's interests at heart."

Try to stay calm and collected, and don't compete with her to demonstrate who cares more for the child. Calmly show her what the baby can do now. She may then be able to appreciate the baby's achievement, too, instead of worrying everyone about it.

"I've tried that with my family. It seems to work while I'm in the room, but if I go out, they start fussing again. Now I either take the baby with me or get them started looking at a book with my child."

Inhibiting Children

"My father-in-law thinks children should be seen and not heard. He expects them to sit still and be quiet even at this age. He keeps saying 'Shhh, shhh,' with his finger to his lips, whenever the baby begins to make a sound. Now the baby just clings to me and won't go to him at all."

Children should be free to express themselves in an age-appropriate manner. Such constant disapproval is not good for the child's self-esteem. Perhaps you can explain this to your father-in-law. Try having him go out with you to the park so that your baby can run around and make noise without disturbing him. Back inside, perhaps he will be ready to look at a book quietly with grandfather.

"What if your child is shy with everybody and cries when he sees strange people?"

Such a child needs support from the parent. You have to tell the strangers that he'll get used to them in a few minutes, that he needs time to "look them over." Hold him very close when you are with new people; this will give him a feeling of security. As he grows older, he will begin to feel more secure with new people.

"Our child is also shy. We know a lady who always asks us, 'What is the matter with your daughter?' Then she pounces on her!"

Tell this woman there is nothing wrong with your child. She is at the stage in which she is wary of strangers but, if given time to get used to them, she will be friendly. Don't be intimidated by such questions. Stand up for your child.

"I have a different kind of problem. When my father comes, he always brings candy. I really don't want my child to have it. Then my father and I have a big argument."

Perhaps you can explain to your father that your doctor and dentist don't think candy is good for the child at this age, and that fruit or crackers would be more appropriate.

"When my parents come to look after the baby, they skip her bath and let her stay up an hour later. Then she seems cranky the next day. When I suggest that they follow my routine, they say, 'Oh, it won't hurt her every once in a while.' It makes me not want to have them again."

Life is much easier when parents, grandparents, and baby-sitters all follow about the same routines with a child. On the other hand, if it is only occasional, and if the child really enjoys her grandparents, it may not be so bad. Having a good time with the grandparents is very important in building a relationship with them. Parents should try not to be disapproving of grandparents' care. Within reasonable limits, children can accommodate some variations in routines. If the baby gets back to her schedule after a day or two, there may be no harm done. Children derive security from following routines, but there should be some flexibility.

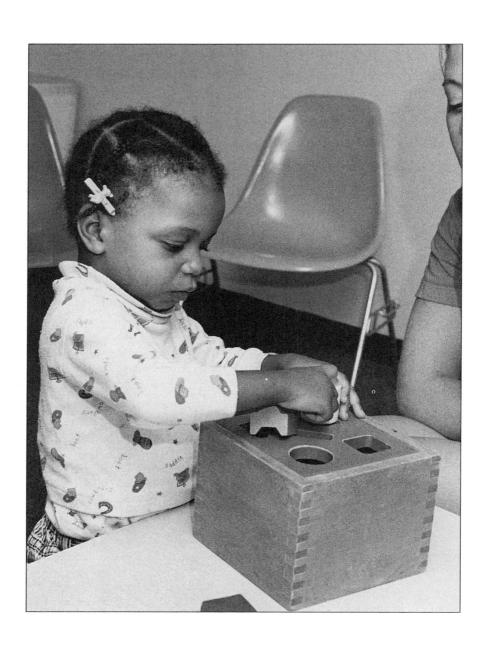

5

The Changing Family Structure

A Father's Involvement

The father's role is undergoing many changes. In some families, the mother works outside the home and the father assumes a bigger share of parenting. Some fathers look forward to coming home to their children and assisting in their care. Other fathers are too busy working long hours to be able to participate, or may feel this is not the father's role, and leave all of the child rearing to the mother. Some mothers welcome having little assistance in child rearing and with their daily decisions. Other mothers become upset over their husband's refusal to participate in the care of the children. They may be concerned not so much for themselves but because they feel children need a relationship with their father in order to be able to establish their own identity. Many fathers do not realize how important their role is and how much they can contribute to the child's development.

Now that the children are entering their third year, have you fathers noticed any difference in your relationships with them and how you spend time with them?

"I travel a lot and don't have much time at home, but I have noticed a remarkable change in my daughter. She's more of a person. She can say more. I find I can relate to her better now, and I feel we are more of a family."

"I don't travel but I have long hours, so I see my son mostly on weekends. He can now tell me more and do more. We can throw a ball to each other. If we take a walk, he points to things on the way and listens to what I tell him."

You are noticing advances in the children's competence that are making it easier for you to relate to them. Some mothers are concerned that the children are not getting to know their fathers and that both father and child are missing something valuable.

"I used to tell my wife that she could have our son until he was five. Then he would be mine and I would take him over and lead him to be a man.

But now I'm glad I didn't wait. When I come home, we all have dinner together. My wife gets him ready for bed, then I tell him a story. On Saturdays, he helps me wash the car or some other job."

Many fathers believe that small children are a mother's concern, that it is not the father's role to tend to the needs of infants. If they are tired when they come home, they feel, the children should be in bed so they can have dinner in peace.

Times have changed. We have learned how important it is for parents to be available for their children's sense of security and trust. Children of both sexes need the experience of relating to both parents, because parents serve as models of what it is like to be an adult man or woman. In some instances, mothers have to go to work while children are very young. Fathers are needed to help in child care and share in household chores. That is changing the family situation.

"We both work, and we have a housekeeper during the day. My wife comes home before I do, so she has her time with our son before I get home. When I come home, he has his time with me. Our time together is spent in having a bath and getting ready for bed. While I do that, my wife is getting our dinner ready. Then we take turns reading to him and putting him to bed."

"I work a late shift and my wife goes to classes in the morning. We've shared in our child's care and the house chores from the start. It's been hard at times, but a good experience."

Importance of Play

"We aren't able to arrange our lives so equally or have help at home, so we take our child to a neighbor, who cares for her till one of us can come for her. We find we haven't been spending time in play, just in the business of making a living, eating, sleeping. Is it important to play?"

All parents need some form of relaxation. Play is also very important to children. It is their work. They learn about the world through play.

"How do you find time in a busy day for play? How much time should you spend at play?"

Every child needs time during which he or she gets undivided attention. The physical care that a child needs takes a great deal of time, and some parents feel that it takes up all of their available time. However, the time spent in relating to a child in meaningful play can be effective even if it is no more than fifteen or twenty minutes a day.

"What is regarded as 'meaningful' time with a child?"

Meaningful time is time the child spends doing something special with you, whether it's playing with you or helping you, going to see something with you or being read to by you. Some parents and children enjoy doing something active; others enjoy a quiet activity, such as listening to music or drawing. These times spent together form lifelong memories and shape attitudes toward parents.

"My contact with my son is just play. We race, play ball, or play hide-and-go-seek. My wife says that I am simply a playmate, that I don't involve myself in anything serious like discipline or teaching."

While it is important to have a friendly, playful relationship with your child, that should not be the full extent of contact. A father is a model of what a man is and does and should at least participate in establishing the same standards of discipline as the mother. He should also view himself as the child's teacher, advocate, comforter, supporter, and caretaker. He, too, can feed, dress, bathe, and put the child to bed when he is available to do that.

"In our family that is just what we have to do. We both work. We discussed this arrangement thoroughly before we had our child. Although I agreed intellectually that that was best for us, it seemed a little awkward and unnatural at first. I was raised in a very traditional family. My father was waited on by my mother, and he had little to do with us. I resented that as a child and missed my father's attention, so I was determined not to be the same. When I got used to taking care of the baby, I got over that awkwardness and felt closer and closer to him."

We are beginning to understand that parents exert more influence on character development by the example they set than by admonition. Studies show that the father who is kind, loving, and involved is more apt to have children who are well motivated than is the cold, distant, autocratic father. A father who can bathe and feed his child does not lose his masculine identity; nor does he lose it if he vacuums the floor, does the laundry, or shops for food. What he shows is that he cares about his child and can take care of him. Does the mother lose her identity if she works outside the home to help support the family?

"I fully agree. I do what needs to be done when I'm there and my wife does it when she is there. I think our child knows who is his mother and who is his father, and I think he trusts both of us."

A child observes not only what parents do and say to him, but what they do and say to others as well—particularly each other. The way his parents talk to each other teaches him how a man and woman relate to each other. These are important steps in socialization for a child.

In more and more families, the mother has to work outside the home while the children are still very young. Consequently, parental roles are being redefined and the family structure is changing. Each family has to make accommodations that suit its individual personalities, cultural standards, priorities, and economic situations.

"This discussion has forced me to look more closely at the role of fathers. It has made me recognize more fully what my role is and what it can mean to my family if I don't assume all aspects of the role. It makes me feel more important than just a checkbook or a live-in baby-sitter."

That's a very good conclusion to this discussion. As your child grows and matures, your role will enlarge and become even more challenging and interesting.

The Single Parent

We have been discussing issues that are of concern to all families. However, because of special circumstances the very same issues may affect a family more intensely or differently. Specifically, I am referring to the single-parent family. Does anyone have concerns on this subject that they'd like to share?

"I'm a single parent by choice, and I work part-time. I've enjoyed being a parent, but it has been hard. I have two worries. One is to find the right caretaker for my child when I am working. The other is that I am doing my job in addition to that of being two parents. Am I shortchanging my child?"

Having proper child care is a concern for most working women.

"My real worry is what my child is missing without a father. Can I do the job of both parents?"

A boy needs a male role model to develop his identification as male. A girl needs to know what an adult male is like, so that she can later choose an appropriate mate. It is important for both sexes to have models of how a man and a woman relate to each other and how they fulfill their roles as parents.

"In order to supply a male image, would having male baby-sitters be appropriate?"

Some mothers of boys have used male baby-sitters. However, these baby-sitters are usually of high school or college age and are not available for long stretches of time; thus, it's difficult to establish a real relationship. An alternative solution is a male relative, like a grandfather or uncle who lives close by and can be in contact regularly. Male teachers in nursery schools and preschool programs can also serve as role models, as can a neighbor, a family friend, even the family doctor.

"It is hard to be divorced and a single parent, but I have done it. The problem comes at visiting time. I try to avoid conflict with my ex and to present him in as favorable a light as I can, because I don't want my daughter to grow up being afraid of men. From some of the remarks my child makes after a visit with him, I suspect that he may not be as careful in what he says about me."

This issue takes on significance no matter which is the custodial parent. Both parents have to keep the welfare of the child in mind and not use the child as a vehicle for hostility.

"As a divorced woman, I am no longer invited to participate with my married friends in the dinner and theater parties. My social life, except for family affairs, is nil. I don't have money to throw parties myself or go to the theater. Or to pay baby-sitters either, for that matter, if I should go out."

All single parents find they need to reorganize their lives on less money. This is often difficult. Many communities have recognized the difficulty and have established social and self-help organizations, such as "Parents Without Partners" and "Kindred Spirits." Some churches have also taken steps to alleviate this problem, and many single parents form less formal associations on their own.

Separation

"Since I am the only parent, my son doesn't like it when I have to leave him. He accepts staying with the sitter when I go to work, but he hates it when my mother comes over on the rare evening when I go out. When he sees her coming, he cries and clings to me and says 'No Grandma,' but he likes to go to her house. He makes me feel so guilty for leaving him."

We have to remember that all children of this age are still learning to cope with separation and the fear that a parent may not return. Their ability to separate waxes and wanes. Even so, parents are entitled to have some time for themselves and need not feel guilty for taking it. You should assure the child that you'll be back in a little while. You can say that when you return, you will come in and kiss her good-night. Or you can remind her what you will be doing together the next day.

Dating

"What happens if I start dating again? The child of one of my friends was very unpleasant to her dates, interrupted their conversations, and wouldn't go to bed. I wonder if it is best not to meet a date at home."

It is not a good idea to meet a new date at home. A parade of dates can be upsetting and confusing to a child. The child may feel threatened by this person who seems to be taking mother away each time he comes. However, if it is to be a relationship of some duration, the person can be introduced to the child gradually. Perhaps you can take the child on a short outing to the park or to an ice cream parlor. Perhaps you can arrange a visit at home and introduce the person to the child's toys.

"What about having a date spend the night?"

That is something the parent has to decide. It depends on how comfortable you feel with the situation and how accepting the other person seems to be with your child. If it is to be a permanent relationship and the person is going to live with you, a child should be told that and whatever questions the child may have on the subject should be addressed. For example, the child may ask where Daddy will sleep when he comes home. The child should be reminded that Daddy is not coming back, that he is living elsewhere, but that he is still the child's daddy. Then the child should be told just what the new friend's role will be. This explanation may have to be repeated many times before the child gets accustomed to the new arrangement.

"If I ever find myself in that situation, I would like it to be without any feelings of jealousy on anyone's part."

That is the ideal situation. It helps if the parent and new partner can remember not to exclude the child, and at the same time not allow the child to dominate the situation so that the new relationship is not jeopardized. This is not easy; it requires understanding of the issues and good communication.

The Death of a Spouse

"I am a single parent for a different reason. My wife died a few weeks ago after a long illness. Since then I've been home with my son trying to do all the things his mother and I used to do with him. Now I have to go back to work, but in view of the big loss he has suffered, I am worried."

He may have more reaction than usual to your leaving for work now. It would help if you could work part-time for the first few days or weeks before returning to work full-time. It is important that the person who takes care of your child be someone he knows, likes, and trusts.

"We are lucky, because our old housekeeper will be coming back. She knows his routine well, and I will come home as early as I can to be with him for dinner and to put him to bed. But he has been wanting to come into my bed during the night. Is that all right?"

Coming into your bed is part of his needing to be sure you are really there. He may need to do that until he feels more secure. You can return him to his bed and reassure him that everything is all right and that you will see him in the morning. Eventually he will sleep through the night again.

"I don't have any urge to socialize except with members of my family and close friends. I want to be with my son now as much as possible. Friends call and invite me out, but I have no desire to go unless my son is included. I suppose that's natural."

It is natural to feel that way so soon after a bereavement. However, you should try to return to as normal an existence as possible. This is important so that you don't unwittingly become dependent on the child's company and actually keep the child from developing his autonomy. This sometimes happens when a father dies and the son is told he is the man of the house and should take care of his mother, or when a little girl is left with her father and told to take care of him.

Whenever one parent has to assume a double role, a reorganization of life is called for. Single parents have to marshal all their resources and support systems in order to cope. The increase in the number of such situations is making the issue of single parenting one society will have to address and meet with trained homemakers, good day-care and after-school programs, recreational facilities, and flexible work arrangements.

Preserving the Mother's Mental Health

Many mothers report that the constant demands of childcare, the inability on most days to have just a few minutes to themselves, is an overwhelming strain. Many of these mothers have the added pressure of keeping house, as well as trying to continue a meaningful relation with their husbands and maintaining a social life. Some mothers complain that fathers do not understand how pressure-packed her day may be.

We have been discussing children's needs, mothers' quality time with them, and fathers' time with them. Now it's time to discuss mother's feelings—and how she feels she is getting along, what things bother her, and what can be done to help her.

Demands on Mothers

"Do I ever feel that things need improvement! I try to keep in mind that I shouldn't shout, but our son comes into our room so early in the morning that I yell 'Get back to bed.' That starts the day off wrong. I need all my sleep."

"Sleep—that's my biggest issue too. Our daughter is so active now that I can't wait till her nap time. I use it to lie down and read a book for twenty minutes. That is my time. It revives me, and I can get through the rest of the day in a good mood."

"I've been talking to other mothers, and most feel that this period has been more difficult than the first year. It's a comfort to know it's not just my child; they are all so active and don't nap as long. That bothers me, because we have such a big old Victorian house that I need the nap time to get work done. I can't spare the time for rest. My husband is so proud of the house that I just have to keep it in order. He spent so much time restoring it."

It is good that the child's nap time is used for mother's rest or reading time. A mother's job doesn't have formal coffee breaks or lunch periods, so she has to take her breaks when the child is asleep. Some mothers make housework a top priority and try to accomplish it at that time. While that may be satisfying for those mothers who find they enjoy cooking or cleaning when not disturbed by the child, most women also need to rest to recoup their energy.

Maintaining Other Interests

"It does take a tremendous amount of physical stamina to keep up with my son now, but that doesn't bother me as much as the need to get away and talk to people on another level. I like talking to other mothers about the children, but I also need to talk about politics, art, literature—all the things that interested me before the baby was born. A chance to do that once in a while keeps me sane."

Every mother should make time to resume some of her former interests. It's a very important health measure.

"I feel a little guilty doing that. I have no family nearby to take care of my son for a few hours. I don't want to impose on a neighbor, and I hate to spend money on baby-sitters, because money is tight."

That feeling is understandable. A parent has to make the decisions that fit best with her circumstances. However, many of us put our emotional health last. We have to remember that we can do a better job as parents when we are rested and in a good mood. That contributes to the entire family's well-being. It may make the difference between enjoying the parental role and always feeling deprived of needed rest or stimulating adult activities.

Let's say a mother had a job she liked and had the opportunity to socialize with people she enjoyed. Now she is home caring for the baby and the demands of the household. She often wishes she could see her friends, but she never arranges to do any of the things she used to enjoy. Her child, who is going through the stage of testing autonomy, announces one day that she wants to wear a party dress to play in the sand. Instead of saying firmly, "This is a dress for a party" and putting it away, the mother gets angry and can't think of a way out of the situation. She is tired and stale on the job; she and the child are in an unhappy mood, and the afternoon is a disaster.

"You've just described my house! That does happen when I'm tired. I've been having a high school girl come in after school for about two hours twice a week. It's a good playtime for the baby and a relief for me. I rest or do something I haven't been able to get to. That little period helps restore my sanity."

Every mother should make time to converse with another adult occasionally. There are many demands on her; she needs help and some time for a break. In any office there are coffee breaks, which increase the efficiency of the work. Likewise, a mother's efficiency and ability to do things increase if she has a break from her routine. It's mental health insurance for the whole family. If a mother needs relief, it does not mean that she is not a good and loving mother.

Fathers' Ideas About Mothers' Role

"The thing that bothers me most is that my husband puts a higher priority on a neat, smooth-running house than on the care of our child. He thinks that simply because our son is bigger and can play alone, I can see to the house full-time.

"I get the idea that most men think being home is a snap. You go to the park and out to lunch, the baby naps, and you have a ball. Later you go out again and come home, and somehow the shopping is done, the dinner is cooked, the baby is bathed and fed, the laundry is done and sorted, and the house is clean—and all this while spending most of the time just chatting in the park with your friends."

"I asked my husband what he thought about my day, and he said, 'Well, both kids arrive in the bedroom about seven A.M. They spend some time with you and some time with me. Then you spend the day playing with the children, taking them out, and feeding them. Then we may meet and all have a hamburger out. Or I come home, and bathe and put the kids to bed while you make dinner.' He left a few things out!"

"My husband does spend time with our son, because I take a course. Recently he announced, 'It's hectic, tedious, and boring, but less boring than it was when he was younger. He's now at that age when he's always wanting something different to do. So that's kind of interesting. But he's always at you for something.' "

If a father spends time alone with his child, he can establish a closer relationship with the child and get a better idea of what a mother's job is like.

"It certainly worked with my husband. Someone asked him about my being home with our son instead of working, and he said, 'It's very important at this point for her to stay home. Hers is a full-time, very necessary job. I can be replaced much more easily than she can.' "

"I think that if I were to characterize my job, I'd say, 'It's all right if you can make the child your sole priority, but when you put another priority in front of him he feels the effect of this.' I have a cleaning woman do the kitchen and the bathroom, and I can enjoy my children while she cleans."

You have to give the children your high priority, because they need your attention so much of the time. It's the housework that has to be done somewhere in between that interferes.

"What I find irritating is never getting one thing finished. I start the dishes, then suddenly I am interrupted, so I leave the dishes and go to help the children out. When I have settled them I pass by the beds and get started on that before I get back to the kitchen."

It is possible to involve your children in helping you to get the housework done. They can help you put some things away. Many children like to be involved in housework this way.

■   ■

"I'm beginning to do that more and more, and it really works, although it may take a little longer to get things done. There's less calling me away from what I'm doing."

Mothers Working Outside the Home

"My problem is a little different—and a little harder because I have a nine-to-five job besides my job as a wife and mother. Although my child is taken care of during the day by a sitter, many of the daily chores are left to me. From my point of view, all of the adult contact during the day doesn't make up for the time I'd like to spend with my child, and there is so little time for it."

"I have a nine-to-five job too. The only reason I can make a go of things is that my husband helps so much. He helps shop and clean, and takes his turn with the baby. We can't do much socializing, but we figure we'll get to do that when the baby is older."

Each family has to organize its life in a way that suits its needs. While the mother at home has problems of isolation, the mother on the outside has the problem of having the outside job plus a good part of the home job as well.

Mother's work is never done. Throughout history in many parts of the world, mothers have been required to do more than take care of children. In North America and in most European countries, the mother's function has been to remain at home to care for the children while fathers worked outside the home. Father's job was to support the family, mother's to care for him and the children. In recent years this arrangement has changed. The cost of living has increased to such an extent that two wage earners may be needed in a family. In addition, many women have been educated to engage in the same careers as men and the women's liberation movement has caused many to reassess their needs. More and more of the child care has been left to others than mother. In this country, about 50 percent of mothers of children under the age of three work outside the home. Of course, that does not mean that they are entirely free of the responsibility of child care or home care. How are those of you who are working outside the home getting along? How do you feel about your situation?

"It is a very mixed situation for me. We both have to work. I like my work, but I feel torn when we leave in the morning and our son cries and doesn't want us to leave. I know he likes our sitter, who has been with us for two years. But it is upsetting to both of us."

"I have just the opposite situation. We drop off our daughter at the sitter's and she doesn't give us a backward glance. Although I am glad she isn't unhappy, I find myself wishing she would show some sign of not wanting to part with me. My husband says I should be glad she doesn't cry."

We have been concentrating on how the children cope with separation. But parents can have trouble dealing with it, too. Many mothers are uncomfortable about leaving their children, even for an occasional night out. Separation is an issue at any age. There is much research being conducted on the effects of separation on children. The effect on parents needs to be studied as well.

Mother Substitute

"I am a computer programmer. I felt that if I didn't keep up with all the new developments, I would never be able to reenter the field later. So I made the choice to continue working. My problem isn't separating, but getting help for coverage while I am working. We had our child in a very well-run day-care center with flexible hours, so if I worked late she could stay there. The problem came when she was sick. When that happened, I had to stay home. Naturally, my employer couldn't put up with all these absences, so I had to find someone who would take care of her at home when she gets sick. It took weeks to find someone suitable."

"I had the same experience trying to find the right person to take care of our son. I found one who turned out to be fine, but her salary almost equals mine. So, from a financial standpoint, it doesn't make sense. I've been thinking about giving up my job until my son is older and I won't need so much help."

"It isn't only the salary that bothers me, but keeping my caretaker happy so that she will stay and I won't be left in the lurch. When I come home, instead of playing with my child I start to make dinner—something the caretaker will like. When she is away weekends, I do things around the house I'm afraid she'll think are not her place to do. I never relax at home with my family."

Finding satisfactory substitutes to care for children is becoming more and more difficult. In the past, members of the extended family could lend a hand, but the extended family has largely disappeared. There has also been a decrease in the number of people entering the labor market as housekeepers or child-care workers. Although the salaries in this field seem high to many working mothers, they are still not high enough to attract a great many capable people. So when a decent helper is found, a mother can become a slave to the help, in order to keep her happy. A great deal of reorganizing of our social institutions regarding working hours and child care will have to occur before the problem is solved.

"I don't get a salary. I get a wage. I can't afford hired help. When I take our son back from the baby-sitter, I'm torn between playing with him and getting dinner ready and the house straightened. I usually end up playing. As you pointed out, he doesn't cling so much if I play first. I then get my chores done more easily."

When a mother comes home from work, children clamor for her attention. No matter how much there is for her to do, it will get done more easily if she tends to the children first. There have to be compromises. In such families it is normal for dinner and bedtime to be later. The schedule has to be different. A well-kept home may no longer be top priority. Perhaps straightening up can be done once a week—after the children are in bed. When they are old enough to help, the children can assist. As more and more mothers work at paid jobs, more fathers are learning to lend a hand with child care.

Missing Milestones

"What has bothered me is that I missed all of my daughter's 'firsts.' My mother discovered her first tooth, heard her first words, and watched her take her first step. I guess I was jealous of my mother. She had her turn with her children."

"I had the same feeling about missing all the 'firsts.' I sort of wished my sitter would let me make the discoveries and think they were the 'firsts.' "

"That was my feeling too, and then I got hold of myself and said, 'You ought to be glad she is interested enough to notice these things. That shows she is on the ball. It ought to make you more secure and happy about leaving your child with her.' "

Many mothers—and fathers too—find it hard to miss being present at the achievement of their children's developmental milestones, which can be one of the most enjoyable parts of parenthood.

"Because of that I stopped working. I realized that this chance to be there with the baby would only come once. We needed the extra income, but I decided to do some belt tightening and make up for the financial loss later."

Jealousy of Caretaker

"I don't worry so much about missing the 'firsts.' What bothers me most is that someone else will be winning the baby's love. I worked hard on establishing a bond by holding our daughter in the delivery room and nursing her for six months before I went back to work. When I come home each day, it seems she is just as interested in the baby-sitter's leaving as my coming home. That upsets me, even though I'm glad she likes the baby-sitter."

"I've had that concern, too, but not about the sitter. My husband works at home, so he takes care of our son when I am at work. When I come home, my son seems to be so comfortable with his father that he doesn't relate as much to me as he used to before I worked."

A child establishes a closer relationship with the person who takes care of him most, because that person is fulfilling his daily needs. If that relationship is a happy, affectionate one, the child will develop trust in that parent. However, that does not mean that the bond to the other parent is broken.

■   ■

"It is so hard to adjust to the fact that you have to work out a different way of being a mother. Is it different if a child is in day care or at home with a baby-sitter?"

Whether the child is at home with an individual baby-sitter or in family day care or a more formal day-care setting, when the mother is reunited with her child she needs at first to devote her time exclusively to the child. Household chores can be postponed until the child feels comfortable and assured that she is home to stay. Then she can start a chore in which she can also engage the child. It enhances the relationship if there is some special activity that they do together and that the child can look forward to, such as having a snack together, reading a story, or playing a game. These activities should be repetitive and predictable, so that the child develops a sense of consistency and continuity.

Time for Parents

"I gather that consistency and continuity are the key words. But it seems to me that there is no time left for working parents to have any life together on their own."

"We waited so long to have a child that we don't mind spending all our free time with him. We take him wherever we go and don't go places he is not welcome. Once in a while, I get the urge to have dinner out with my husband, but he won't hear of it. He is a home person."

"At first we felt that way, too. Each of us had to travel frequently for our jobs, so we felt that we were cheating the baby if we took time off for ourselves. But the baby is almost three, and we feel we have given her a good start. Now we are beginning to schedule a little time off for ourselves together."

All parents need time to be together alone. Everyone needs some refueling time. The job of parenting can be done with much more enthusiasm when such time is arranged. Parents who work outside the home are just as entitled to this time as other parents.

"The hard part of setting up time for ourselves is that everything is a project. We have to plan and arrange for sitters well in advance, because they are not always easy to get."

The situation is indeed complex. Our society has not yet begun to make the adjustments necessary to take proper care of the children of working mothers. Perhaps a change like paying mothers to stay home to take care of their own children during the first three years is in order. In addition, parenting groups, where mothers at home with their children could end their isolation and all parents could learn more about child rearing, could be offered.

■   ■

The Relationship Between Parents

Most of our discussions have centered on the needs of the child. But the relationship between the parents is also important. Everyone likes to feel that the arrival of a baby enhances the tie between parents. This does happen, but the relationship between parents can become strained if they neglect each other in their concentration on the baby.

Do you feel that your relationship with each other as husband and wife has changed since the arrival of the baby?

"I think that my husband feels our son is now my top priority. He under-stands that the baby hasn't taken away my love for him and that my feelings for him are entirely different than those for the baby. But he sulks a little when I have to interrupt what we are doing to attend to the baby."

Competing for Attention

"I know that my wife pays as much attention to me as she can. But I still miss our discussions and the time we spent alone. In that way, yes, I think the baby interferes. Even so, I get a kick out of watching our son and the excitement he shows when he sees me. So I guess it's a trade-off."

"It works in a different way with us. In my country, the family revolves around the man absolutely."

In this country, that is no longer so. Some of us come from different cultures, and this may add to our difficulties. All families have to work out a way in which members show that they cherish each other. That's terribly important to the mental health of the whole family.

There is no doubt that life is different with a baby. A baby's needs are very time- and energy-consuming for parents. Parents can and should arrange to have some private time with each other. It may be possible only once a week, but it is important to arrange for it and then take steps to carry it out. This can be the beginning of drawing parents together in situations they enjoyed before the arrival of the baby. Parents can then enjoy the time spent with the child without feeling that they have been robbed of their time together.

Father's Expectations

"I think that the real problem isn't just time together, but what the father's expectations are. My husband comes from a family where the father was top priority, and the children knew it. I think a lot of fathers have that view. But families aren't run that way anymore."

At one time many families operated like that. In extended families, a grandmother, maiden aunt, or other family member was available to lend a hand with the children so mother could be more attentive to father.

Hired household help was more available. Even though households today may be smaller and have many labor-saving devices, the need for human assistance is still there.

"My husband and I are aware of the need to have time together. But baby-sitters are expensive and hard to find. So we sort of leave the issue on the back burner."

Mini-Vacations

"It was getting so bad in our house that we decided to hire an off-duty nurse from the pediatric service of a nearby hospital for one night. We checked into a hotel in the evening, went to dinner with friends we hadn't seen for at least a year, and saw a play. The next morning, both of us slept late for the first time in two years! We had brunch, took a walk, went to the museum for an hour, and came home rested, happy, and as anxious to see our baby as he was to see us."

Parents do need to have vacations from their children. You are their primary caretakers and shouldn't separate from them at this age for long periods of time, but you can spend a night out away from them. Nobody stays on a job from morning to night and gets up during the nights seven days a week on and on without some kind of respite.

Changing Roles

It may seem to us that our parents had less difficulty. In some respects, that may be true. The roles of men and women are changing, and that is affecting the family structure. When women viewed being a wife and mother as their primary role and did not have to work outside the home for financial reasons, they were more content to stay home and wait on their husbands and children. When women began to take over men's jobs during the wars, they created new roles for themselves and never could resume the old roles exclusively. Now both men and women are trying to redefine their roles in work, politics, marriage, and child care.

The family structure has to change to adapt to the changing roles. The problem is that children's needs don't change. The number of people devoting time to caring for children is dwindling. Therefore, much of the job falls to the nuclear family, which in many instances is finding it hard to cope. That's why we are so concerned here with helping to improve family relationships. This is a transitional period in society, and we have to help each other find the way that will make for a happy family life, allowing parents as well as children to grow and develop to their maximum potential.

6

Realizing Your Child's Capabilities

Delaying Gratification

When the children were infants, their parents responded immediately to crying. But now that the children are older they are often expected to wait to have their needs gratified. In fact, parents become impatient with their children because the children's ability to wait is so limited. Parents begin to wonder when they will be free to do simple tasks and activities without interference from their child. Now that the children are older, are you finding that they require the same immediate response to their needs as they did when they were infants?

"I'm a little disappointed, because I expected that by now my son would be able to wait better than he does."

At this age, between two and three, children still do not have the ability to wait that adults have. What seem like short delays to us seem like an eternity to a child.

"As soon as my husband leaves in the morning, my son wants to go out for a walk. But I want to do the dishes and straighten the house first. He just can't wait; he cries. Sometimes, just to get some peace, I do take him out. Other times I just can't and we have a lot of unpleasantness and sometimes even a tantrum."

"When I have to wait in a supermarket line with my daughter, she is just impossible."

"My worst moments are when I go to my mother's and I have to stay to help her with some task. My son just wants to get out of there and can't wait to go home."

"Most of us have had similar experiences. Are we expecting too much of our children too soon? Is there some way we can avoid this conflict?"

As children get older, their capacity to wait improves. It is the parents' job to help them by prolonging the waiting time gradually. Actually, we've all been doing it to some extent since the children were infants. For example, when the baby cried for food and saw it being prepared, he learned that it was for him and soon began to be able to wait until it was ready. Later, when he threw his toys down and wanted them back, he learned to gesture for that and waited until the toys were returned.

"Is it possible for a child of this age to wait a half hour until you make the beds, put the dishes in the dishwasher, and put a few things away?"

It is possible to postpone the child's gratification for as long as a half hour. For example, if the child asks to go for a walk before you are ready, you can say, "Yes, we can go as soon as I make the bed [or put the dishes in the dishwasher]. You can help me and then we will go sooner." This works better than a statement like "No, we can't go now. I have to clean the house." In the first instance, you give the child a positive response and something to do while she is waiting. Most children respond to this approach. In the second instance, your response is negative and frustrating, and the child responds accordingly. In the first case, she learns to postpone her gratification. In the second, she doesn't.

"This approach has been mentioned in other situations too. My child was very impatient, especially when she asked for a cookie before mealtime. Instead of saying, 'No cookies now,' I've begun to say, 'You can have cookies right after lunch. Help me set the table and we'll have lunch soon.' That seems to work."

Telephone Calls

A parent who is talking on the phone is physically present but not in communication with the child or able to attend to the child. To the child this is exclusion, and most children cannot tolerate exclusion.

"Well, what should be done? A parent does have to talk on the phone sometimes."

It often helps to include the child by taking him on your lap and telling him with whom you are talking. For example, you might say, "I'm talking to Grandma. I'm telling her what we are going to do today. Do you want to talk to her?" Usually the child will say something and slip off your lap. He has been included, so he is then able to find something to interest him by himself.

"Suppose it's a business call or something else important."

You should try to make these calls when the child is napping. If that can't be done, explain the situation to the caller and proceed in the same way: put the child on your lap and tell him who is calling and about what. It doesn't matter whether he understands the subject. The important thing is that he has been included.

■   ■

"I always try to have everyone call back or leave a number where they can be reached. I tell my family and friends to call after nine P.M., when our child is asleep."

That approach avoids unnecessary problems. Mothers who are on a telephone squad for an organization should try limiting their calling or responding to times when the child is asleep.

Talking to Other Adults

"I have difficulty with our child when I try to talk with my husband or a visitor. Our child can't wait for us to finish a sentence without interrupting."

As with telephone conversations, the child feels a need to be included. If the child is initially included in the conversation, she will either sit with you and make a remark or two or become interested in a nearby toy which she can play with. The time parents can spend conversing is increased if they direct a remark or two to the child.

"I like to read, and I especially like to keep abreast of the news every day. When my son seems engrossed in a toy I may pick up the paper and try to read. But that doesn't last long. He spots what I am doing and won't let me finish."

That is another activity the child interprets as exclusion. Again, if the child is taken onto the parent's lap and told what she is reading about, he may quickly get down and go about his business. Serious reading should be postponed to a time when the child is asleep.

"I find not reading as much and when I want to to be the hardest part of parenting."

It is hard even for many adults to postpone gratification. So imagine how hard it is for a young child with an immature central nervous system to postpone gratification. Remember, delay of gratification is a learning process and is achieved slowly.

Transitional Objects and Self-soothing Behaviors

Many parents find it upsetting to see their child carrying around the remains of a blanket or teddy bear, or sucking their thumbs or reaching for a pacifier. It is important to understand that these are normal activities, the child's way of controlling her environment when she is lonesome, bored, a little anxious, or tired. These activities substitute for the comfort received from mother at an earlier age. Are any of you disturbed by such behavior? How do you deal with it?

"My son still carries around an old piece of blanket. It seems to satisfy him as much as the whole blanket used to. He won't allow me to replace it with a new blanket."

How do you feel about it? Aside from washing the blanket, which showed your feeling about its smelly, ragged condition, did you say anything?

"I've told him he must leave it at home when we go out because he might lose it, and he accepts that. But I dread the scene if we should lose it. Once we left it at his grandmother's house, and we had to drive back to get it. He cried all the way."

"When my son finishes a bottle of milk or juice, very often he won't give up the empty bottle. He carries it around, and sometimes goes to bed with it. Friends and family tell me to simply take it away from him, but I don't because he got so upset the one time I tried. When he is busy doing something, he drops the bottle, and I can take it away without any problem."

A child of this age begins to experience times when every need is not met and tries to satisfy the need himself. He may thrash about and his hand may touch a bottle, a soft blanket, or a soft toy left in the crib. This object may give him a pleasant sensation like he had when mother supplied something that he needed. So instead of crying for mother whenever he feels the need for a pleasant experience, he tries to overcome it in a way he is able to do himself.

"Can that mean that the mother has failed in some way?"

Mothers can't be available for every need every minute. There are times when an infant has to wait. Parents may find that holding a certain stuffed animal or edge of a blanket soothes a child and will offer this to the child without realizing that the child may become dependent on it later.

"Do all children do this? Is it a necessary step in their development?"

Not all children need to comfort themselves this way. However, it is common. In the literature on child development, favorite toys and objects are referred to as "transitional objects." So they have achieved a place in scientific observation.

"Should children be allowed to form such attachments?"

In most cases, it is not a matter of allowing it to happen. These attachments usually happen spontaneously, except when parents initiate or reinforce the attachment because they want to quiet a child.

A parent who sees that a child seems to need the toy or other object only when he is bored or lonesome can engage the child in some diverting activity. Parents can read a book with a child; engage him in playing with a ball, building with blocks, or listening to records together; or even arrange a visit with another child.

There are many things that may upset children or make them anxious—overly enthusiastic visitors, strange places, noises, other children, and animals, for example. It is important for parents to recognize what bothers their child, then be available to him for closeness and comfort, so the child won't feel the need for the soothing objects.

"Suppose you let a child form an attachment to an object. Will he ever stop on his own?"

When these objects no longer fulfill a need—as the child becomes more competent and more occupied in play with others and with school activities, for example—these objects are given up. Parents are sometimes impatient to have them relinquished before the child is ready.

"What about thumb and finger sucking? Shouldn't more strenuous measures be taken about that because of the effect on the teeth?"

Taking strenuous measures, such as scolding the child, taping the fingers, or painting fingers with a bitter substance to discourage sucking, are all counterproductive. Parents have to remember that being able to put a finger in the mouth is one of the earliest exploratory activities of a baby; it provides her a way of giving herself the first pleasure of which she was aware—sucking at the breast or bottle. Part of the parents' job is to help her find other satisfactions as she grows. In general, the same things that lead to use of a transitional object—fatigue, boredom, loneliness, and anxiety—lead to continued need for satisfaction in thumb sucking, so the same remedial procedures apply.

"When do children give up these objects without parental encouragement?"

Most children give up these objects between three and four years of age. However, it may take some children until they are five. Others relinquish these objects by the age of three, or when they enter nursery school.

"What about the child who continues to use a pacifier?"

A child who continues to use a pacifier is not attempting to satisfy a sucking need. A child who has had the pacifier stuffed into his mouth to keep him quiet may use it as a transitional object. It is used under the same circumstances—fatigue, boredom, loneliness, and anxiety—and should be dealt with in the same way as any other transitional object.

Safety Issues

Fearing they will be labeled "overprotective," some parents are reluctant to take safety precautions where such caution is called for—such as at a swimming pool; at a lake or ocean; or on a trafficked street, where children of mixed ages are playing without supervision. There is a difference between setting limits to help ensure safety and inhibiting the child's natural exploratory activities—such as using a slide or swing in the park, riding a tricycle, running, and climbing over an obstacle. Parents deal with

■   ■

these situations differently. Have you ever been called an overprotective parent?

"My husband is always telling me that I am too anxious—that I see danger in undangerous situations."

Water Safety

"Last weekend, we went rowing on a lake. Before we got into the boat, I put a life belt on our daughter. Later, she wanted to take it off. Her father let her, even though I protested. Then she leaned over the side and almost fell out, but we both caught her and almost fell out ourselves."

"We have that all the time with our son. He wants to go in the water without a life jacket or water wings, and I won't let him. His father feels I'm making a 'sissy' out of him, that I should let him take chances."

"In the summer we spend a lot of time at a community pool. We stay in the shallow end, but I can't be sure my son won't stray too far away. So I insist on a life jacket, even though I'm one of the few mothers who does. Other mothers tell me I'm overprotective."

No parent wants to be called anxious or overprotective. However, in certain situations safety precautions must be taken. Most water areas for young children have strict rules—and for a good reason. A parent should not rely on a child's judgment or self-control. It is much better to institute precautions consistently than to be giving children mixed signals about safety.

Street Safety

"Now that he can walk, my son doesn't want to hold my hand or be strapped into his stroller. We live on a busy street, and I am afraid that he may run off before I can stop him. So I insist that he hold my hand or else get into the stroller. This sometimes causes a scene, and I wonder if I'm being too cautious."

"I let our son walk to the end of each block alone, and he waits for me at the curb. Then I hold his hand and we cross together. I think he knows he has to wait for me."

"I can't do that with our daughter. The minute she is out of the stroller, she is off and running and I have to chase after her. I wouldn't dream of trusting her judgment."

We want to teach our children to respond to our limits and we want to feel we can trust them. However, on a busy street that is quite risky. It is the child who waits who poses the more difficult problem, because a parent can't be certain that the child won't be lured into the street by something like a ball or brightly colored paper, or become so absorbed in walking that he forgets to stop at the curb. At this age, the child still needs close supervision.

■   ■

"But children have to have someplace where they can be on their own."

That is true. It can be accomplished best in a park or on a quiet side street. If this is made a regular event, the child learns that when mother says "When we get to the park [or other landmark]," he will be given freedom to walk and explore.

"When can a parent expect children to understand to be careful of traffic?"

This varies with the maturational timetable of each child. A general answer is when the child is verbal and can understand the danger involved.

Playground Safety

"At the playground, older children sometimes take over where the little ones are playing. Some of these older children are very considerate, but others are very vigorous and boisterous. The little ones may get hit with balls thrown too hard, poked with shovels, or banged with bikes. When that happens, I stand close to my child and ward off these kids. That causes comments such as 'Don't keep him such a baby' or 'Let him grow up.' "

"That happens to us too, even when we go visiting and there happen to be older children. Then I'm really in a spot: he doesn't want to leave, and he can't participate safely."

Parents of children this age have to intercede by organizing turns in activity or by playing with their children in such a way that the older ones will want to participate too. Some children who have been maltreated by older children may themselves become "bullies" when they get older. Others may be inhibited in their social development if they are not protected in these situations.

"What is the real meaning of the term 'overprotective'?"

Overprotectiveness is generally understood to mean the inhibition of age-appropriate exploratory behavior. For example, a parent who keeps a child who is just learning to walk strapped in a high chair or stroller and doesn't permit her any freedom on the floor for fear she might fall is being overprotective.

"Our children are at the stage where they want to climb up and down the slide in the park. I am afraid to let my son do this, so I avoid going to the park as much as possible. Am I being overprotective?"

Children of this age need to engage in activities that develop large muscles. Climbing is one of these activities. Allow your child to climb, at first while he holds on to you and the rail, and then to be there to catch him when he comes down. Then offer recognition of his accomplishment. As he practices and becomes more proficient, give him less assistance but still be ready to steady him. In time, you will be more at ease when he climbs.

Safety in the Home

"My son wants to climb on everything. He tries to climb the bookshelves. I'm afraid he will pull them over and I stop him. Is that all right? I'm not home during the day, because I work. My housekeeper, who has five children, says boys will be boys and that I should let him."

Of course, if there is a danger that the shelves will topple over, your son should not be allowed to climb on them. Perhaps the housekeeper can take him to a playground and let him climb there, where safer climbing opportunities are provided.

Some communities have special gym classes for young children that provide activities for large-muscle development. Many rural areas have fences, trees, and hills that are ideal for climbing. Some parents set up climbing areas in the home—ladders fastened safely to walls, for example.

"My boy loves to run. He's still a little clumsy and he falls, so I'm constantly saying 'Not so fast,' 'Be careful,' or 'You'll get hurt, so slow down.' Once he fell and skinned his chin on the pavement, and it was a long time healing. I guess I have fears of his being permanently disfigured or breaking an arm or a leg. Some of my friends think I am overdoing it a little."

Perhaps you are conveying some of your anxiety to him, and as a result he is a little inhibited and lacking motor control. If you are so worried about his running on the pavement, perhaps you can have him run in a grassy area where spills won't be so traumatic. Running is part of a child's normal development at this age. Fortunately, the bones of children this age are more pliable and breaks do not occur as often as one might fear.

Certainly, the parents' job of defining limits for safety and allowing enough room for development is not easy. Furthermore, what may be right for one family may not be right for another. However, there are certain guidelines for water safety, traffic precautions, and playground situations that are common sense and can serve for most people.

Manners

Naturally, parents want their children to have good manners. They want their children to greet and part with people properly, to use utensils instead of their hands, to be perfect hosts, to take turns, to share toys, to sit still through meals, and to refrain from interrupting when adults are conversing. The children are older now, but they are still not mature enough to act this way consistently.

We have discussed manners before. We were wondering if this issue is still a concern and if so, how you are coping.

Table Manners

"Our daughter isn't so good on the cup by herself, but she does manage with the spoon now without putting it in her mouth upside down. Once in a

while she gets a little impatient. She tries to get food in her mouth with her hands, and winds up smearing it all over herself. I simply wipe the food off and let her try again. She seems to be making progress."

"My child eats only food she can hand-feed herself. She has completely given up the spoon and fork, although she was getting the hang of feeding herself pretty well. So I give her just what she can pick up by hand. She is very fastidious; everything has to be dry and neat."

Most children this age are learning to use a spoon. Some have begun to use a fork, although it is often abandoned temporarily. Some can manage with a cup. In general, the children are more competent with utensils than they were at age two, but they are still a little messy.

Modeling Manners

"I can't see fussing about table manners. I'm satisfied if my daughter gets her food down, because she is such a poor eater. Isn't it true that in time all children begin to eat the right way?"

In general, that is true. If parents and other caretakers model proper handling of utensils, children will follow suit as they become more competent. Many children respond to comments such as "Mommy and Daddy hold our spoons this way" and "You hold your spoon all by yourself very nicely" or a similar expression of approval.

"Don't you have to correct them each time so they will remember? My husband and I have a tendency to do that."

Repeated correction sometimes has the opposite effect. It may make eating too problematic and cause some to lose interest in eating. You have to recognize what helps your child the most and what level she has achieved. Some children are very responsive and have matured enough to want to emulate the parents in this way.

"I've been trying for a long time to get my child to say 'please' and 'thank you.' Am I jumping the gun a little?"

It is good to say "please" and "thank you" to your child and as a model for him when you speak to each other. If sometimes he says either "please" or "thank you" in some form such as "ta" or "tata" first, recognize that he has said it and then say, "That's nice" or a similar comment.

"My friend's son is the same age as my son. The other day, she was insisting that he say 'please.' After several promptings, he began to cry, so she just gave him the juice. I wouldn't have done that. Am I too lenient or is she too demanding?"

Simply modeling and providing approval and recognition when success is achieved is a more effective approach. Dissatisfaction felt by a parent may be conveyed to the child, who then has a loss of self-esteem.

■   ■

"Does the same principle apply to greetings and good-byes? Sometimes I try to make my child say good-bye to a visitor. He complies only once in a while. Should I just say it myself in the hope that this will stimulate him to do it when he is ready?"

That is usually the best approach. If you are not expecting compliance, you do not convey a feeling of disappointment to the child.

"But what about people who give you the feeling that there is something wrong with your baby or the way you are bringing him up?"

The important issue to remember is your child's feelings and his relationship with you. Perhaps you can reply for the child while holding his hand. This includes him in the greeting and may encourage him to offer his own greeting.

"I don't care about strangers, but it bothers me when Grandma says, 'Johnny doesn't say hello to Grandma?' "

It may help if the reply gives the visitor the idea that you are working on the issue. You can say, for example, "Yes, we're working on it. Pretty soon he'll be saying hello by himself."

"It isn't just visitors and grandparents. I wonder what methods my sitter is using in this area. When I came home the other day, my sitter was returning with my daughter from a stroll. The sitter was trying to make my daughter say 'good-bye' to a neighbor, and was critical when the baby didn't respond."

It is difficult but necessary to find out about baby-sitters' methods and have them deal with issues your way. If they are literate, you might provide them with books about child rearing in a tactful way. You can say, "Here is a book that explains our ideas about children. Maybe you'd like to read it sometime and see what you think of it." In some places there are courses for caretakers in which your caretaker may be willing to be enrolled.

Dining Out

"My husband and I used to go out for dinner several times a week. Since our baby was born, we've tried to go out at least once a week—primarily to give me a change of scene. But restaurants have become very expensive, and now there is the cost of a baby-sitter. So last week we decided to go with our son to a fast-food place. He wouldn't sit still. Is it too much to expect them to sit through a meal quietly now?"

"We've gone through the same thing with our daughter. The first time we went to a very fine French restaurant that we had always liked. It was a disaster. The next week we tried a nearby Chinese restaurant. They welcomed all of us, brought a high chair and a few paper toys for the baby, and served the meal quickly. Between tastes of rice and Chinese cookies for the baby, we managed to enjoy ourselves."

■   ■

"I don't care where we go, as long as it's out! So we've settled for a nearby hamburger joint. It's quick. Our baby chews on a bun, some meat, and even french fries. There is a lot of hustle and bustle, so he doesn't have to be so quiet and we don't get embarrassed if he stands up or climbs into our laps."

As some of you have found out, children of this age are not ready for a formal slow-service dinner in a restaurant. It is best to pick places where the food is served quickly and children are welcome. Most children are able to manage for as long as they are eating. If given a toy, book, or crayon and paper to amuse her, the child may remain seated twenty minutes to a half hour.

"What if the child is still restless and wants to walk around?"

If that happens, the parents can take turns walking with the child to different parts of the restaurant—the lobby, a window, or the cash register, for instance. The child may then be able to sit a little while again back at the table. Perhaps he can be offered some dessert or some milk. A great deal depends on the time of day—whether the child is being kept up past a nap time or bedtime. The lighting in the room can make a difference—what adults consider romantic lighting may seem dark and scary to a small child.

Of course, the child's hunger level is also a factor. If he has just been fed at home, he will certainly show no interest in eating and sitting still. If he is very hungry, he will not be able to wait. It is a good idea to carry a few crackers or some bread for the child to munch on until the meal is served. The parents' attitude also can contribute to the child's response. If they are relaxed and in a good mood, things go better. If they are tense, the child senses it and can become tense and restless too.

Sharing

"Our daughter's behavior when we have company is beginning to bother us a little. She doesn't allow anyone to play with her things. If she passes out cookies, she takes a bunch for herself first. It's upsetting, especially if you don't know the visitor well."

Now that the children are becoming more verbal and sociable, parents may expect them to be good hosts and hostesses too. Sometimes a plate of cookies held by both parent and child can be passed around. The parents should see to it that the child has a chance to partake of the cookies. If this is the usual pattern when company comes, the child begins to learn the sequence of events and gets the idea of a host's role. It is quite natural for your child to grab a bunch for herself if she hasn't had her share.

"What about when there are guests and you are talking and the child interrupts? Should you make the child wait?"

"Parents just can't just talk to their guests—at least, not in our house. So my husband and I take turns talking to guests."

Taking turns talking to guests is one solution. Another is to include the child in your conversations. Even if he doesn't understand all that is being said, he may be less demanding. In some cases, it is best to interrupt your conversation to meet a child's need. At this age children are still not able to wait for you to finish, but most can cooperate when the parent says something like "Just a second, dear, and Mommie will get . . . ," then complies with the request. What usually causes problems is that parents exploit the "just a second" and exhaust the limits of a child's tolerance.

Dealing with Special Events

Most children become upset at the prospect of going to the doctor or dentist, or to the hospital. Parents wonder whether to tell the children in advance or to say nothing until the event is at hand. It is also difficult for many parents to decide how much to tell the child. Some parents find this is a problem even when the event is enjoyable, such as a trip, a visit to grandparents or inlaws, a party, or the arrival of a friend. Children may become very excited and anxious about these events as well, and may experience mood changes, or changes in sleep and eating patterns. Are you experiencing any difficulty in knowing when and how to tell your child about an upcoming event?

"I have that problem every time a baby-sitter is due to arrive. I know my son is not going to like having me leave, so I don't want him to be anxious too long in advance. At the same time, I don't want it to be a shock when the sitter arrives. But somehow I never hit it right. He always gets upset when I mention going out."

"If I say 'I'm going' just twenty minutes before leaving, my daughter is upset the whole time. If I tell her earlier than that, she sometimes forgets and gets interested in something. Then she isn't moping when I actually leave."

We should be honest and prepare children for things to come, but timing also has to be considered. For instance, if you are going out for dinner that night, you don't have to prepare the child in the morning. After the child has finished her dinner, you can say, "Mommy and Daddy are going out tonight and your sitter [mentioning the name] is coming to be with you. She will play with you, read to you, and put you to bed. Before you know it, Daddy and Mommy will be back."

"My child always protests no matter what I say."

We can't expect a child to say, "All right Mommy, I don't care if you go out. Have a nice time." Children need to show you that they are displeased. It is normal for them to react in a way that shows their attachment to you and to show some concern about your leaving.

"When my baby-sitter comes in, my daughter is quite unfriendly to her until I leave. My sitter can't understand why the baby isn't happy to see her."

Of course, your child feels more secure with you. Another reason for your child's mood is that when you go away, she is not sure that you are coming back. You have to emphasize that you are going to be back in a little while, perhaps adding that when you come back, you and she are going to do some fun things. Often, whether you have expressed this or not, the child may get the idea that you are annoyed with her, and she wonders if you are going to go away and not come back. Perhaps she has been a little bit naughty that day and you have been displeased with her for something, so maybe—just maybe—you are not going to come back. She does think that way and we have to be aware of how she may think. If you can explain this to the baby-sitter, the sitter may be less disturbed by the child's mood and may try to be more helpful to the child.

"What we do is have a special project under way before the baby-sitter arrives. The baby-sitter then continues with the activity until I am out the door. For example, we'll make cookie dough that is to go into the oven after I'm gone. The activity then becomes more important than the separation."

It's a very good idea to have special games and activities that occur only with the baby-sitter—a record that only the baby-sitter puts on, a toy that is used only when she's there, or refreshments that are enjoyed only by the child and baby-sitter. This makes your leaving a less stressful and more exciting time for your child.

Visits to the Doctor

"We can't seem to solve our biggest problem—doctor's visits. My son is afraid he is going to get a shot each time he goes. Sometimes he does, so I can't promise him he won't when I have to tell him we're going."

Many children get upset at the prospect of seeing a doctor because of the inoculations and testing doctors must do. If you have had this experience with your child, you might try to get him a toy doctor's kit. This allows him to act out a visit to the doctor, and perhaps give "shots" to his teddy bear or doll. He may then begin to feel less fearful of visits to the doctor.

It is important for parents not to convey anxiety to the child. Find out what is going to be done at the visit. Then, about half an hour before leaving the house, tell the child where you are going. If he is to have a shot he should be told. Say that you will hold him, that it may hurt a bit for a moment, then it will all be over. Then tell him some pleasant thing that is going to follow the doctor's visit. On the way, perhaps mention the toys he will find in the waiting room before he sees the doctor and what the doctor will say to him in greeting. You might suggest that he show the doctor how big he has grown since the last visit or ask the doctor to examine one of his toys. In time, the child feels that the parent is not anxious and doesn't deceive him or minimize the hurt the child experiences, and then he gains confidence and may even get to enjoy visiting his doctor.

Visits to Dentist

Dental visits should be started after most of the teeth have erupted in the latter part of the second year. It is a good idea to arrange a "get acquainted" visit before the first examination. A child can accompany the parent at his or her visit to the dentist and watch all the fascinating things that happen: the chair that gives a ride up and down; the water that spins around in the little bowl; the little paper cups.

"We don't have any trouble with that. When I say I'm going to the dentist he can't wait, because he knows the dentist will give him a ride in the chair."

"Should I take my child to a special children's dentist or to a family dentist?"

If you have a family dentist who is willing to take the time to interest the child in proper dental hygiene, that dentist is fine. Many dentists are pleased to do that because this is preventive dentistry. But if your dentist is not comfortable dealing with young children or their special needs you should find a pediodontist.

Hospitalizations

"What can you say to a child this age who has to be taken to a hospital? Our daughter has a squint. The doctor feels that she has not responded to the patch, and that surgery is needed. The appointment is for next week. We don't know what to tell her."

You should explain the process to her in language she can understand. Tell her you know how much she dislikes the patch procedure and that the doctor can make the eye better more quickly if you take her to a special house called a hospital. Tell her that you will go with her (if the hospital you have chosen permits parents to stay). Find out from your doctor what the actual procedure is going to be. When your daughter questions you, explain the steps simply (for example, whether she will be going to the operating room on a stretcher or wheelchair). In the days before her stay in the hospital, she can act this out with her dolls if she wishes to. It is a good idea to describe the way the operating-room nurses and doctors dress and that she will take off her clothes and wear a special gown, too. There are picture books now that show children in hospitals that may be helpful if the real situation cannot be demonstrated. Some hospitals offer a presurgery tour for children. The child should know, too, that she will eat and sleep there and that you will be with her. If she feels assured that you will be with her and she gets a sense of your feeling secure, she will, too. Children are usually made more anxious than they would be by the parents' anxiety.

"Suppose a child has to go to the hospital for other reasons."

The principle is the same. Tell the child the reason and procedure in language the child can understand. Don't provide too many details. Try to answer all of the child's questions, and let her know that you will be there all the time.

Other Exciting Events

"I find that too much advance preparation for happy things like a birthday party sets my child off. He has spells of crankiness and sleep disturbances. So I don't tell him until just before the event."

"When my son knows several days in advance that we are going to visit his grandparents, he whines and wants to know when we are going."

"My daughter just can't wait if she knows we are going to have a visitor, even people she sees often. First she seems happy, then she begins to ask when they will be coming and gets very tense at every sound. Then she pouts, mopes around, and gets cranky. I've learned not to tell her too far in advance."

When you tell children of a visit or other event in advance, it is a good idea to keep them occupied until the event. Children this age have no sense of time, nor do they have the ability to wait for days for an event to occur. They become frustrated and irritable when they have to postpone gratification. They should be provided with an activity while they are waiting. When parents understand this, it is easier to cope with the child's behavior. It is also important that the parent not add to the difficulties by being angry and upset.

"We're planning a trip to California, and we are taking our son with us. We haven't told him yet, but he has not been himself for the past few days. I wonder if he has noticed our preparations for the trip."

Children are very keen observers and very sensitive to changes in their environments. Your child may have noticed that you are doing something different. Perhaps you are shopping a little more, or mentioning the trip during telephone conversations. He may have overheard something and misinterpreted it.

It may help to include the child in your plans. For example, let him participate in getting his things together—his teddy bear, favorite books, and other items important to him. He can be told how you will travel, what you will see, and where you will stay when you get there. He may need to be told the details many times and may ask many questions. These questions may indicate what sort of anxieties he is having and what reassurance he may need.

SECTION II

Age Thirty to Thirty-six Months

*T*he children have made great strides in their use of language; some of them can communicate and understand quite sophisticated concepts. Their ability to separate from mother has increased; some can even visit Grandma's or a friend's house without her. They are beginning to understand the concept of taking turns and are beginning to engage in interactive play with peers. Some have begun to show interest in toilet training or have already achieved bowel and bladder control.

Highlights of Development—Age Thirty to Thirty-six Months

At age two and a half, your child's development may be progressing rapidly. You may find yourself constantly bombarded with questions or continually running after a very physical toddler, and you are probably tired because your child is so inquisitive and active. A thirty-month-old child can walk on tiptoe, jump with both feet, and stand on one foot. She can run rapidly with little or no falling. She may enjoy small motor tasks such as drawing, coloring, doing puzzles, and playing with toys and dolls. When presented with a puzzle consisting of simple geometric shapes, she is able to fill in most of the puzzle and match one or more of the colors. She may also be able to name items in a book that the parent points out and will be able to give the use of some objects.

A two-and-a-half-year-old may begin to refer to herself by pronoun rather than by name. She is helpful and likes to put things away when her behavior is approved. She can carry breakable objects and likes to steer riding toys in different directions. She often talks at length when given a chance, and she may say "Hello" and "Good-bye" spontaneously but not on command. At some point between thirty and thirty-six months, a child may begin to recount an immediate experience.

Because the year between twenty-four and thirty-six months is a time when children struggle to establish autonomy, parents may get cooperation only part of the time. Children may insist on wearing a particular pair of shoes, or "doing it myself," or staying at home when a parent wants to go out, or ordering a friend or parent to "sit here" when playing. They can dress themselves in simple garments, fastening shoes and unbuttoning easy buttons when given enough time and approval. At the table, they are quite proficient at eating with a fork and spoon and can sit for almost the length of the dinner if included in the conversation and serving.

7

Readiness for Nursery School

Some of you have indicated an interest in nursery school programs before children are three. There are many developmental skills children need to acquire before entering nursery school. How ready do you feel your children are for nursery school?

Language Skills

"I wanted to enter my son in nursery school last year, but although he was big and well developed physically, his language skills were lacking. I felt a teacher would not be able to understand him. Now he speaks quite clearly and can form short sentences to indicate what he wants."

"My daughter is very petite and looks much younger than three. But she spoke early and now can express herself very well, so in that area she is ready for nursery school. But I'm not sure about other areas."

Of course, being able to communicate verbally is a very important factor in determining readiness for nursery school. A child who cannot make herself understood may feel lost and abandoned no matter how well developed she is physically. In fact, children who are well developed physically or perhaps large for their age are sometimes expected to perform at an older age level. This often leads to disappointment and may interfere with the child's development of a good self-image. Conversely, the petite child, who is able to communicate even above age expectations, may be infantilized.

Motor Skills

"My son is a great talker, but he is a little clumsy going up stairs because he doesn't always alternate his feet. And he isn't very good yet at pedaling his tricycle.

However, he runs quite well and can throw a ball with pretty good control. Is that unusual?"

Maturational rates for all areas of development differ for each child. In your son's case, the coordination in his lower extremities is a little slow in developing. It may be due to late maturation of those pathways, or to lack of stimulation. Perhaps he has not had sufficient opportunity for stair climbing or pedaling.

A nursery school should offer space for large-muscle motor activity in a gym or playground for children who are ready.

Separation

"I am glad you mention readiness, because although I noticed this before he didn't seem ready in other ways to go to nursery school. So I was comfortable about waiting till he was older."

In what way did you think he was not ready?

"He wasn't able to separate from me. He wouldn't play at a neighbor's house with another child he liked and whom we saw every day. If we were visiting somewhere and I went into the next room, he'd follow me no matter how interested he seemed in his play. I was afraid he'd want me to stay at nursery school with him. In the last few weeks, all of that has been changing, so I'm getting to feel he will be ready for nursery in the fall."

"My daughter was like that until recently. Now she does quite well in familiar places, like our friend's house or Grandma's, but it takes her quite a while to be comfortable in a new place, so I was wondering about a nursery school."

Even if the child does not show obvious feelings of being uneasy in a new place, it is a good idea to visit the school ahead of time. He can see children there and what they do; this will give him an idea of what nursery school will be like, and he may feel more comfortable in the first days.

"I've started walking by the nursery school about the time the children are going home. I tell my child that mothers come to meet their children to go home, and I say 'That's what I will do when you go to school.' Now when we go by the school he says 'My school' and seems pleased. I did that because he had difficulty separating from me to visit anywhere."

Many parents expect children to be able to separate before they are actually ready. How quickly separation is accomplished depends on the temperament of the child and his maturational timetable, as well as the parents' understanding, support, and patience.

Adjusting to Many Children

"I've been wondering how my daughter will react in a group of fifteen or eighteen other children, even though she is doing very well now in her play group of four children."

■   ■

A small play group is good preparation for nursery school, because a large number of children may intimidate a child at first. Nursery schools are aware of this. Many schools start children on different days, so that children are not confronted by the whole class on the first day.

Toilet Training

"While the things we've been talking about are very important, it's toilet training that concerns me most. My worry is that my son won't be toilet trained by three. He shows not the slightest interest in that area."

Not all children are ready to assume responsibility for bowel and bladder control at the same time. Most children will do it when they are ready— usually, around age three. They can then achieve complete control in a very short time—some in a day, others in two or three days, when allowed to do it on their own.

"Suppose a child is obviously not ready when nursery school begins, and you have registered the child and paid tuition?"

You should discuss this with the school officials. Most nursery shools will agree to a release from your commitment or arrange for later admission. The rush to get children into nursery school by a certain date is not always in the child's best interest and puts a strain on the parents as well.

If there are still several months before the start of nursery school, remember that the children may develop a great deal during this time. Development often comes in spurts.

Selecting a Nursery School

"I am not sure what to look for in a nursery school and just how to go about evaluating one."

In selecting a nursery school for their child, parents should find out the teachers' approach to discipline, the ratio of teachers to pupils, and the qualifications of the staff. In addition, they should investigate the physical setup of the classroom—indoor activities, toilet facilities, and outdoor play equipment. They should also look into the specifics of the daily program—whether it is structured or flexible, and whether the school follows a special program such as, for example, the Montessori method. It's helpful if parents see the school in action and observe the class to which their child will be assigned, so that they can become acquainted with their child's future teacher. Watch how the teacher deals with the children, how she settles difficulties between children, how kind and thoughtful she is. Also, listen to her tone of voice, and notice whether she sits close to the children or towers above them, and whether she shows a sense of humor. During the visit, parents should also observe the children.

■   ■

Do they seem to be happy? Are they busy and involved in their activities? Or are they quiet and sad? Do they wander around aimlessly? Are there many group activities, or are the children allowed to follow their own creative bent?

"As a child, I was intimidated by teachers and school officials. I want my child to have a better school experience than I had."

That is understandable. Visiting a few schools, talking to the schools' officials, and asking about programs and approaches may make you less anxious.

"I asked the first school how they dealt with separation. I was told that the mother is allowed to stay with the child the first day or two, but after that the teacher can handle it better if the mother leaves. I crossed that school off my list."

A school that has a hard-and-fast rule like this does not allow for the children's different maturational timetables. However, a child that needs more than three or four weeks to separate may not be ready for nursery school.

Many schools have a teacher make a home visit to get acquainted before the child enters school. In this way child and teacher are not complete strangers on the first day.

Other schools have children enter on successive days instead of all at once, so that the class grows gradually. Some start with a short program of one hour the first day or two, then gradually lengthen the school day to two, two and a half, or three hours.

"Isn't it a little too long to expect them to stay three hours?"

That is a long stretch for many three-year-olds. The tendency now is to extend the school time not because that is best for the child but because this fits parents' needs (since, more and more often, both parents work). It gives the working mother a sense of security that her child is being cared for while she works, and it reduces her need for child care.

"I was wondering about school types and philosophies. Is, say, a Montessori approach better than another?"

Labels don't always tell the story. Parents have to visit the school and see how it operates to determine whether it is the sort of school that suits their ideas and their child. The school's equipment and setup may be adequate, but not the program. Or the teacher may be too casual and not involved enough with the children. The teachers' personalities and methods are more important than any specific label or philosophy.

Emotional Climate

"You seem to stress the emotional climate provided by the teachers. But what about the program itself?"

We feel that having a trained, understanding, patient, empathic, friendly teacher who knows child development and can help a child cope and explore a new environment is far more important than the specifics of a program.

"I am concerned mainly about curriculum—whether there is a set schedule each day or just free play with good and safe equipment. That's important, too, isn't it?"

Certainly how each day is spent is important. There should be some pattern to the day—ativities that follow one another regularly—just as you pattern events at home. This predictability helps a child develop trust in the school and allays anxiety.

However, structure should never be so rigid that children do not have the opportunity to explore, develop friendships with other children, and experiment with different toys.

"You mentioned the playground and gym. What about the classroom itself? I've seen some that looked new and fully equipped and others that appeared a little beat up."

A school should have certain essentials—small chairs, low tables, low shelves stocked with blocks, appropriate dolls and doll furniture, stoves, play dishes, and puzzles. It also should have drawing and painting materials and equipment for motor play. Some schools have dress-up equipment for imaginative role playing, real kitchen setups, tricycles, doll carriages, even roller skates.

A parent should look into how much choice children have in selecting areas of interest. Some children may only want to build with blocks, others to cook all the time, and still others to ride tricycles. How does the teacher encourage them to try other activities? How does she deal with sharing? How does she help the child who is left out by the others? How does she teach respect and care of equipment? How does she model communication? All these aspects of the school and teacher should be considered.

It is also important to notice what kind of group activities there are and how the children participate. Do the children gather willingly for storytime? Is there a time for looking at books individually? Does the teacher sit down with one or two children while some others gather around? Are other children permitted to continue with their own interests?

"It sounds as if there is a lot for teachers to do. I know in some schools there is a main teacher and some assistants. What should be the proportion of teachers to children?"

The ideal ratio is one teacher to four children. Most schools manage one teacher to six children and some one to eight. Some states require one teacher to five for this age. Parents should investigate the role of the assistant teachers—how they relate to the main teacher, to each other, and, of course, to the children.

■   ■

"We are musicians, so we are concerned that some form of music appreciation be included in the nursery-school curriculum."

Music in some form—dancing or clapping to rhythm, playing in a rhythm band or singing, for example—is an essential experience and should be part of any nursery-school day. Listening to records and telling stories to the music is done in some schools.

Hygiene

One area that we have not yet mentioned is hygiene. How clean and well kept is the school? Are things in their place? Do the bathrooms have low sinks and toilets? Do the children go to the bathroom by turns? Are they accompanied by an adult?

Parents should also look into the question of children attending schools with colds or other infections. What immunizations are required? Is there a nurse available? What first-aid equipment is there? Who is trained in use of this equipment?

"I'm curious about snack time in nursery school. I don't allow my child to have sweets, so what can I do if sweets are offered at the school?"

Snack time is an important activity for children of this age. It is a time during which they learn to take turns and to serve others. They may also begin to learn about proper nutrition. If you are encouraging your child to develop certain eating habits, you may be able to arrange with the school to have your child given a certain food during snack time. Of course, you will have to supply this food. The essentials of good nutrition are being given much more attention at nursery schools now.

"Should only large, formal nursery schools be considered? What about informal groups run in homes for just a few children?"

These groups have a lot to offer as well. They can give a child more individual attention in a less intimidating environment. There may be less equipment, but there may be more imaginative use of the materials that are provided.

Nursery School Interviews

Some parents have begun or are soon to begin nursery-school interviews. Some schools request psychological evaluations prior to consideration for admission. Some parents worry that it may be harmful to the child, others are afraid something negative may be discovered. Many parents wonder how valid such a test can be for a child of this age, and whether tests given at this time can foretell the behavior of a child when he or she actually begins nursery school.

"When we submitted our nursery-school application, we were told we must have our son tested. I was surprised and upset. I thought they must have

discovered something wrong. I later found out that some schools routinely require such testing. What do they expect to find out about children who are this age?"

Many schools that require this testing believe it helps to have some objective standard by which to measure applicants. It has been found that most children of a certain age respond to standardized questions in a particular way. The ones that do respond within the expected range form the groups from which the school makes its selection. This method can help make the selection more uniform.

"When I asked about these tests, I was told that they are used to avoid the criticism that selections are made on too personal a basis and to avoid favoritism to certain children. That made me feel a little more comfortable."

Anxiety

"Can these tests be harmful to a child in any way? It seems to me that they can be very upsetting at best."

Of course, no physical harm can come to the children as a result of testing. But some children are made anxious by the unaccustomed situation as well as by the stranger who administers the test.

"My neighbor's daughter was too upset by the situation to cooperate in the testing. My neighbor said she wouldn't subject her child to it again, even if she lost the money she paid."

"I have friends whose children thought it was a game and seemed to enjoy it."

The tests—and the environment in which they are administered—are designed to minimize adverse responses. Many children, if properly prepared, respond to the testing as a game. Some are fatigued by the length of the procedure, so testing is frequently done in two sessions.

"Is there any preparation for these tests, like special games or books?"

There is no special preparation. By this time, the children have been stimulated in motor and language activity. They have had practice with puzzles and building toys, as well as with activities such as riding a tricycle, jumping, and climbing. They can relate to peers and adults appropriately for their age.

"Aren't there some factors that affect the outcome of the test? I've heard that some children are asked to come back to repeat the test."

Certain factors can affect a child's performance on the test. One of these is the emotional state of the child at testing time. For example, any disruption of routines—a visit to grandparents, visitors at home, not sleeping well the night before the test, or an angry confrontation with a sibling or parent—can upset a child and influence the child's performance. Parental anxiety or undetected onset of an illness or cold prior to the test can also have an effect.

Another factor is the setting in which the test is given. For example, the building in which the examination takes place may remind the child of going to the doctor's and may upset him. Examiners are aware of this possibility, so most have the test-site offices decorated in pleasing colors with appropriate pictures and children's furniture and a few toys to put the child at ease.

The personality and appearance of the examiner may also affect the child. The examiner should be trained to approach a child pleasantly and to present himself or herself in a way that will entice the child to want to participate.

Advance Preparation

"Should a child be told in advance about the test? If so, how?"

Parents should tell the child less than twenty-four hours before the test that he is going to a special place to meet a person who will talk to him and play games with him. It is important to add that the parent will be there with him.

"What if your child asks why he has to meet this person?"

The child should be given an answer that explains the reason as simply and matter-of-factly as possible. The child can be told that he is going to see a person who knows about schools and will be able to determine what kind of school would be best for him.

"Aren't there some schools that don't require formal evaluation? The school I'm taking my son to makes admissions decisions based on an interview and on observing the child in a classroom situation. What are they observing?"

There are many good schools that do not require prior testing. A trained person observes the way the child walks, talks, plays with toys, and relates to her. She notes his attention span, his level of anxiety, and how he responds to frustration. She tries to determine the child's grasp of simple spatial and visual concepts. The child may also be invited to a classroom to see how he interacts with other children.

"Suppose he clings and won't do anything he is asked at that time but would really be ready at three. How would the mother and school know that so long in advance?"

There is no way to predict how a child will develop. However, interviewers are aware that children can mature a great deal between two and a half and three years of age, and they make certain allowances.

"Isn't the testing a better prediction?"

It has been found that no testing done on children younger than three years had predictive value. Admissions decisions based on an interview and detailed history are as reliable as those made after formal testing. No test alone can give a full assessment of a child. Other information— family history, impressions of adults close to the child, observations of the child's behavior at home and play, and interviews with the child—are needed.

8

The children's communication skills are improving. Their sentences are becoming longer and their ability to express complicated concepts is increasing. They are beginning to use more prepositions, adjectives, and adverbs. Some parents are finding that their children are ordering them around and they begin to feel that the children are controlling them. They also notice the way their children talk to other children. They are afraid they will upset their friends and then won't have friends.

What have you been noticing about your child's speech development?

"We are thrilled because our son is saying so much more. We were worried, because we both work and he was home with a housekeeper who didn't talk much. So we made a point of spending more time talking with him and reading to him when we came home. Maybe that helped, and maybe he was not ready until about a month ago, when words just seemed to pour out and then little phrases like 'Mommy home,' 'Din all gone,' and 'Baby go bye-bye in ca'age.' It's not perfect, but it's coming along and we are so happy with his progress so far."

You are right, it is hard to say which was the more important factor. As we have said before, it is usually a combination of the child's maturational timetable and environmental stimulation.

Stages of Speech

Children's acquisition of speech comes in stages. We were all pleased when the children began to name objects and people, and even more so when they began to say phrases and three-word sentences. As their sentences become more complex, children begin to make announcements: "I came in my car" or "I came in a taxi," for example. Later, they begin to give directions to each other: "Put the doll in the carriage" or "Don't read." They speak to us this way, too, and we may be offended because it sounds like a command. But this is only a stage in speech development—an imitation of the way we speak to them, perhaps—and will gradually give way to a more conversational, interactional form of communication. The children will begin to show concern for one another and for the reactions they receive. They will be asking permission and raising more questions, such as, "I take the shovel, okay?" or "You play with me?"

"I must have talked a lot to my son, because he is doing a lot of talking. Sometimes he just orders me around. He'll say, 'Let's go home now' in a very commanding way. I don't know whether to laugh or be angry."

"My daughter calls to me and says, 'Momma, come here this minute.' Maybe that is the way I sound to her. In a way it's amusing, but I don't want her talking that way to others."

Of course, the tone of voice a child uses may be an imitation of a parent. Most children go through a stage of commanding. However, they are not as dictatorial as they sound. They are simply expressing themselves, and we are the ones making that interpretation.

"Sometimes I hear my son talking to himself as he plays with his blocks. He'll say, 'Put the car here. Go slow.' Or he'll say to his car, 'No, no, don't go there.' Is that unusual?"

That is not at all unusual at this age. The children's language has improved to the point that they talk aloud as they play. They are really thinking out loud.

Collective Monologue

"I've begun to notice that when we have one or two children playing together in our house they don't actually talk to or play with each other most of the time. They will each be playing with something, and each will seem to be describing what he or she is doing without the slightest attention to what the others are saying. Once in a while one may glance at what the other one is doing, perhaps making a comment (but usually not), and then going on with his own thing. They don't seem to be really playing with one another. Is this part of this stage too? Should I intervene and try to get them to play together more?"

"I've noticed that too, and though it seems an odd way to play I like it because it keeps a group of children quiet when they are playing in the house."

To an adult this behavior may seem strange, but it is a normal stage. This level of development has been given the name "collective monologue" by language-development experts. Each child seems to be conducting her own monologue in the company of other children, and requires neither an audience nor input from others. Parental involvement here may interfere with the child's fantasy or her way of working through issues of interest to her. It is much better for the parent to be a silent observer.

■   ■

"You learn quite a lot about yourself if you listen. The other day I heard my little girl scold her doll: 'Sit down and be quiet! Let Mommy talk on the phone.' That got to me, because I didn't realize I did it so often or that she was upset by it."

"I heard my daughter say to her doll as she put it into the doll bed, 'Don't cry, Mommy be back soon' over and over again. I began to think perhaps she was reassuring herself as much as the doll. She doesn't cry now when I go out, but she used to. Maybe that's how she got over it."

Until now, the children have been observers, taking in everything adults do and say. Now they are becoming more expressive. Parents should observe closely the way their children are expressing themselves now, and use those observations to better understand their children.

Cause and Effect

"I've been wondering how much they really understand what we say. I try to reason with my son. For example, I explain to him why he has to hold my hand to cross the street or why we mustn't leave the refrigerator door open. But it doesn't seem to register at all."

"That's just what I've been wondering about. When I give a careful explanation, either he doesn't understand or he doesn't try. Maybe he simply doesn't listen."

"I think they don't listen. I know my son does not. He seems to be too impatient to get on to the next thing. What can I do about that?"

A child is not yet able to understand cause and consequence unless she has experienced it many times. Remember how many times the children had to throw something off the high-chair tray until they understood the consequences of their actions? Even now they may try to throw things out of windows or down toilets. They can't foresee the consequences.

"But we tell them, and it doesn't seem to matter. I give a whole lecture about something and it doesn't matter."

Consider this example: Johnny runs across the street ahead of his mother. She goes after him, grabs him, and says, "You must hold mother's hand. A car might have come along, and the driver might not have been able to stop in time. He might have hurt you, and you would have had to go to the hospital. That would make Mommy and Daddy very sad and you would have to stay in the hospital a long time."

The mother should simply have said, "You must hold mother's hand crossing the street. Cars can hit you." Many parents make the mistake of giving involved explanations before a child is ready for those explanations. Children need a short statement consistently repeated until they have absorbed it.

"I think I know what you mean. A week or so ago while we were out walking, my daughter pulled her hat off her head. I said, 'It's a cold day.

■   ■

You'll catch cold and be sick and have to go to bed. You won't be able to go out to play and your friends won't be able to come and play with you. You might have to take medicine . . .' and on and on. But she would not keep her hat on. A few days later she did get a cold; whether it had anything to do with the hat I don't know. All I said was, 'You didn't wear your hat. Now you have a cold.' She just gave me a long look, and from then on she hasn't removed her hat when we are outside."

Because of their limited experience, it is very difficult for children to respond to lengthy admonitions. As parents, we try to protect them from experiences that we know are harmful; that is our job. But it is also our job to try to tune in to their level of communication. They have made great strides this past year; a few have even reached a conversational stage. In a few more months, their conceptual capacity will have made even greater progress.

Fantasy Versus Reality

Another area of concern to parents of children this age is how to interpret and understand their expressions of fantasy. Parents sometimes mistake fantasy for lying, or worry that the child can't distinguish reality from fantasy. Are your children expressing some of their fantasies to you?

Lying

"I have a question about lying. This morning my son said, 'Mommy, I did poo in the potty.' When I asked him to show it to me, he said, 'No, I washed it away.' I didn't know how to react. I quickly changed the subject, because I didn't want to give him the idea that he could get congratulated for something he didn't do. I hadn't started encouraging him to use the toilet, so I don't think I gave him any reason to want to please me."

This is a common dilemma for parents, and it should be handled very sensitively. It's best to be nonjudgmental, so that you don't give an innocent child the feeling of distrust or one who is telling a story a feeling of not being believed. You can say in a nonconfronting tone, "Oh, you did? Well, next time please let me see, too." Notice that I said "telling a story." Children of this age are not lying in the sense that we use the term. That is, they are not telling a falsehood with the intent to deceive.

Parents have to remember that a child of this age cannot tell the difference between what he would like to have happened and what really did happen. In other words, he has difficulty distinguishing reality from fantasy. Sometimes a child is so eager to have something occur that he begins to believe it really did and reports it that way.

Imaginary Friends

"My daughter has an imaginary friend. At times I think she knows that she manufactured him and that it's a game, but at other times I am not sure."

■   ■

"My son also has imaginary friends. He tells me long stories of what they are doing or going to do. Should I go along with him and play up the fantasy, or should I tell him he is making believe?"

You should accept the child's fantasy and go along with it, while letting the child know that you know his friend is not real, but that it is all right to make believe.

Let's suppose you are sitting down to lunch and your child says, pointing to your chair, "Not there, Tommy is sitting there." You can say, "Oh, let's make believe Tommy is sitting over there," then, pointing to another chair, "He is having lunch with us and I will sit in my chair." Before your child can protest, you can quickly divert his attention by saying, "What do you think Tommy likes for lunch?"

"When I try that approach, my child always protests that the imaginary friend is 'really real,' and I get nowhere!"

You should let your child know that you understand how much he would like to believe his friend is real, because you know how much he would like to have a friend playing with him right now. Tell him it's all right to make believe. In that way you make him comfortable with his fantasy, yet aware of it.

"I'm having a hard time getting my daughter to understand the difference between real and make-believe. How can I help her?"

Sometimes it helps to switch roles, to make believe you are the child and that your child is the mother. The child may pretend to dress you, comb your hair, or feed you. Then you can revert to your real roles and say, for example, "Now, I'm going to be the real mommy again, because I have to make our dinner so we can have it ready when Daddy comes home and you are his real little girl. No more pretend."

If your child protests, you can assure her that you can play make-believe again. Mention a specific time, so that she understands that you mean it.

"My son pretends a lot, but I know now when he is pretending. When it's something he wants to do he uses the word 'someday.' 'I'm going on the tramway again someday,' or 'I'm taking a helicopter someday.' "

"My daughter is not like that; she is very unpredictable. The other day her grandmother asked where we were going. My child piped up that she was going to a party. Grandma asked, 'What party?' My daughter answered, 'My birthday party.' Annoyed and surprised, Grandma said, 'It's not your birthday.' "

Children do a lot of wishful thinking. Seeing Grandma may have evoked a wish that she was going to her birthday party. After all, Grandmas are known to give presents for birthdays.

Dreams

"What about dreams—a dream that they really believe happened?"

Children sometimes have dreams that are so vivid they believe they actually happened. A child may wake up at night disturbed by a dream. The parent should reassure the child that it was only a dream, that it didn't really happen, and that you are there to take care of them.

Tall Tales

"You seem to be saying that all that a parent need do is gently point out what is real and what isn't. I'm worried that if I take this approach with my son, it will be easy for him to slip into outright lying when he is older."

"I get flack from my parents that I'm too accepting of the things my child tells me and that he'll grow up to be a liar. I remember having my mouth washed out with soap for telling a lie, but I don't want to resort to that."

"At what age can children tell what is real from what is not? When does a tall tale become a lie?"

A child may have difficulty distinguishing between reality and fantasy until the age of five or six. Parents have to continue to help children make this distinction. Punitive measures like washing the mouth out with soap or spanking may encourage the very behavior the parent is trying to stop.

"I can still hear my mother's voice: 'Tell Mother the truth. I'll be able to tell if you are lying, so don't try it.' Or: 'Are you sure you're telling the truth?' I hated that."

When parents are aware of the level of the child's development, they understand that the child is confusing fantasy with reality and that she has to be given help to understand the difference. These are difficult concepts and the child needs time to be able to learn to deal with them. Most children brought up without accusations of lying do not resort to lying later on. This takes patience and understanding on the part of parents, but it helps in a child's later moral development.

Whining

Many children go through a period when whining is one of their primary coping mechanisms.

Some of you have recently made comments about whining. Is whining still a concern for any of you?

"My daughter doesn't whine often, but when she does it upsets me. I used to say that if I ever had a child I wouldn't permit whining."

"My daughter whines quite often. I tell her to stop, but that just seems to make things worse."

Telling a child to stop whining usually does not work. For some children, whining is a way to deal with situations that are difficult for them. If a child has been told not to cry, whining may be a kind of compromise between a cry and a demand.

Causes

"When I have answered what she has asked me for the twentieth time, I explode. At eight o'clock this morning she started saying, 'I want to leave for the park' I said, 'Not just now, in a few minutes' and she just stood there whining. It has happened a lot, and I have lost my patience and I'll say, 'I don't want to hear you saying it again and if you are going to keep asking, go in the other room.' I know it's wrong, because it doesn't work."

It is not unusual for parents to respond in that way to whining. Some parents sometimes add a warning threat, such as "If you don't stop whining right now, we won't go to the park at all." That approach may only worsen the problem.

Children this age have little sense of time, so they may become anxious and impatient when they have to wait. Whining is their way of coping with situations they can't control.

One way of dealing with whining is to reassure the child. You can say, for example, that you know she wants to go to the park and that you will be going very soon. You can suggest that she get her toys ready, or help you with whatever chores you have to finish before you leave. Most children respond well to this approach.

"My daughter sometimes asks for candy or a treat right before lunch. Instead, I give her something to do and ask her to help me make lunch. She is so busy that she doesn't have a chance to whine. Then, right after lunch, I let her have the candy. Since I've been following this routine, she's cut down on the whining."

"My son sometimes wants to be picked up when we are walking. My husband gets annoyed with him and tries to ignore him. So my son begins to whine. I decided to pick him up as soon as he asks and let him know it is okay. That has cut out the whining, and now he asks to be picked up less than before."

"I've noticed that my child begins to whine just when I begin to talk to someone on the phone or when I'm busy doing housework. Why does he pick just these times to whine for something?"

Close examination of the situation may reveal that the whining started only after the child made a request that went unheeded.

Delaying Too Long

"Maybe that explains our situation. We've begun remodeling the house we are living in, and we try to get a project done each week. Since we began

this schedule, my son's whining seems to have increased. I guess I've been too busy to notice the first time he calls for something."

"Does that mean parents should stop whatever they are doing the minute a child wants something?"

We have been saying that children of this age are *beginning* to be able to delay gratification, and that parents have to help them by increasing delay in small increments. One of the causes of whining is delaying recognition and gratification of the child's needs beyond his level of tolerance.

Ignoring

"My mother says that the way to break a child of whining is to ignore him when he whines and to give him attention when he stops. But I just can't ignore my son's whining, so I eventually give in."

Your mother is following a method that some people in the child-development field advocate. Their theory is that a behavior will be stopped because when it is not noticed, it will be extinguished by lack of reinforcement. This can happen. However, this approach can give a child the message that no one cares, and may cause him to give up easily when faced with a challenge. He may also become angry and demanding, or withdrawn and depressed. Your mother's method can stop the whining but the accompanying responses may be more undesirable. A parent should try to assess the causes of the whining and deal with them as they occur.

Appropriate Attention

"Isn't whining just a way of getting attention. If so, should we be encouraging that? My mother says, 'He just wants attention so just leave him alone.'"

There is nothing unusual or unhealthy about children needing or wanting attention; it is characteristic of this level of development. The parents' job is to try to satisfy the child's needs in a way that is consistent with the child's level of development. As we have said, some children respond to challenging situations by whining. Others cry or have a temper tantrum or just give up. We are not trying to devise methods of punishment for a child's need for attention.

"I have found that our son whines when he is tired and just doesn't know what he wants. If I'm not tired, too, I can cope with it and do something quiet with him, or even get him in for a nap or to bed early."

Of course, parents get tired too. They have moments when they can't summon up all the good parental qualities they have when they feel fresh and rested. It's good that you recognize that the child's fatigue, as well as your own, can cause whining.

Regression

The children have been making progress in many areas. However, there may be occasional setbacks that cause parents to feel there is something wrong either with the child or with their child-rearing methods. Has this happened to any of you?

Feeding Themselves

"My son, who has always been independent and has been able to feed himself very efficiently for many months, suddenly asked me one night to feed him his dinner. At first I didn't know what to do. It was such a switch from his usual way that I did it without saying anything. The next day he was feeding himself again."

This sort of regression is usually transitory. It often occurs when the child is tired or has recently witnessed a younger child being fed. The child may want some of the attention that is being bestowed on the younger child. He is giving a message that he feels left out. If he is told to feed himself, it may make him feel that being able to feed himself leads to being left out.

One way to handle this situation is to acknowledge that it must seem nice to be a baby and be fed again. Then feed him without further comment, but make favorable remarks when he does something more age appropriate, like helping to put toys away or drinking from a cup.

Carrying

"My son has been walking since he was eleven months old, but every once in a while he still wants to be carried. I had gotten to the point where we didn't need to take a stroller with us on walks. But I never know when he'll ask to be carried, so I've begun taking the stroller again. Is his behavior unusual?"

On the contrary, it is quite common. The novelty and wonder of being able to move on his own has worn off. He may realize all of a sudden how large the world is, and feel a need to be safely held and carried, as he was as a baby. Sometimes children are simply unable to keep up with the parents' pace.

"Should they be picked up? They are older now, and harder to carry. When I try to put my daughter into her stroller, she kicks and screams and won't get in."

They should be picked up and held to reassure them that you are there for them. Perhaps you can try walking a few steps holding them until they are soothed, then quietly say, "You are such a big boy/girl that I can't hold you anymore. Let's get into the stroller and I'll wheel you." Some children are satisfied when this approach is used.

■   ■

"At first, I thought there might be something wrong with my child's feet, so I took him to the doctor. Then, when I found there was nothing wrong, I got angry and scolded. That did absolutely no good."

Scolding is rarely a good response. It is better to try to figure out why the child needs something that he seemed to have outgrown, then respond in an appropriate manner.

Accidents

"Is it unusual for a child who has been toilet trained to begin having accidents again? We had no problem training our son. In fact, he was able to control both his bowels and bladder in just a few days. Now he has more accidents than successes, and we don't know what to do."

This is usually attributable to change in the child's routine, such as an illness, a move, or the arrival of a new baby.

"We did have a baby, but that was two months ago. It didn't seem to bother him at first. But I have noticed that he constantly watches me change her. I heard this could happen, but I thought it would be sooner."

When a new baby arrives, an older child may be envious of all the attention lavished on the baby—such as diaper changes. It is a good idea, therefore, to try to notice the older child's more mature accomplishments, so he will continue to feel that it is worthwhile to be the older child.

"We went on a vacation and were away two weeks. Our daughter seemed to enjoy the overall change, but the change in toilet facilities upset her and she wet herself several times a day. When we got home, she was okay in two or three days."

"My child has a bad cold and had to be on medication and forced fluids. He began to have accidents too. As soon as the cold subsided, he got full control again."

These are both examples of the surprise and anguish parents experience when they aren't aware of the consequences of changes in daily routines.

Sleeping

"The change that bothers me most is the change in our son's sleep pattern. He was finally sleeping through the night, and now he gets up again two or three times."

"My daughter also did that for a few weeks. Now it's over and she is sleeping again. She cut two molars during that time. I didn't think that teething kept children awake at this age."

Teething may be a problem for children who are cutting their two-and-a-half-year molars. When this is over, they return to their usual sleep patterns. Children who have had a very active day or whose daytime

■   ■

activity is too tiring may also have difficulty sleeping. Parents who are aware of this can change the child's activites.

"I know that is our problem. I am on the go all day, but I guess it is too much for our son. I've noticed that when we spend the day quietly at home he seems to go to bed more easily and sleeps better."

"My son used to go to bed without any fuss, but lately we can't get him to fall asleep. He calls for us and climbs out of bed. It reminds me of the early months, when we had to rock him to sleep."

As a child gets older, his sleep pattern may change—including the time he is ready for bed. So if his bedtime is changed accordingly, this problem may be overcome. Some children begin to play more vigorously with their parents before bedtime. Going to bed can therefore become a difficult separation from fun and family activity. Parents should give children a quiet time before bed, so that the separation will not be so difficult. For example, reading or some other routine can make children more receptive to the notion of going to bed.

"I think playing too vigorously before bed is our problem. Both of us work, so we like to have a good time with our son when we get home. I guess we can't expect to get him to bed as early as we did before without giving him a cooling-off time."

"Our child used to be so sociable, always wanting to play at other children's houses. Now she only wants to stay home. Is this unusual?"

She may have had an unpleasant encounter away from home. She may be unable to express this verbally and is trying to cope with the situation by avoiding it. However, this may be only a stage in the separation process; she is regressing because she needs time to redevelop the ability to separate.

Parents should remember that maturation does not progress steadily but rather by stops and starts—regression and progress.

Separation

We discussed separation early in the year, when the children were just two. When the children pass two years of age, parents may expect them to separate without any protest. But children at this age are not verbal enough to understand that the parents will return; they still have no concept that the parents exist even when they cannot be seen. Some parents have difficulty putting the children to bed and don't realize that removing a child from pleasant play with Daddy or Mommy is an interruption as well as a separation. Children have to cope with separations of varying degrees several times a day—at the end of play time with parents and at bedtime, for example.

Have you noticed any difference in your children's reactions to your leaving them or their leaving you?

"My son is able to accept his father's leaving every morning, but he is still inconsolable when I leave. Sometimes it gets so bad that I'm tempted to go back."

Children may get used to one parent leaving on a regular basis, but when the second parent leaves that may be harder to take, because it becomes a separation from both parents.

"I made the mistake of coming back once or twice. That only made it worse—there was twice the amount of crying. Now I say, 'Good-bye, be back soon.' I leave quickly, and my mother or the baby-sitter quickly gets him involved in some activity. They tell me that he stops crying very quickly and seems happy."

It is best not to prolong the parting, and to say "good-bye" and "be back soon." The child should be told at what point in his day you will be back—"when you are taking your bath" or "when you come home from your walk," for example.

Loud Protests

"As my daughter gets older and bigger, the crying is so much louder and more vigorous and the clinging so much harder to avoid. It has become harder for me. I feel so sorry for her."

The loudness of the crying at separation is not always in proportion to the child's feelings. The children who cry the loudest may be the easiest to divert, while the children who are less demonstrative may be more affected by separation.

"Does that mean we really shouldn't leave our children at this stage?"

Children do need constant physical closeness to their mothers—at least until they are three, and often longer—before they separate comfortably. In our culture that kind of child care is not always possible. Our children are required to accommodate themselves to this situation—and they protest. We are trying to help parents understand children's needs and to deal with them as best as possible, without feeling there is something wrong with the child or with themselves. In some primitive societies, children are always close to their mothers or an assigned mother. Our children are primitive but our society is not. That is the issue.

"This is such a sensitive issue. What should be done when we do leave a child?"

One thing is parting quickly without making a big issue and emphasizing your return. Another is to say something like "It is time to . . ." and then say "This is Mommy's time to go to work (or to school, to visit Grandma, etc.)." In addition, it is important to tell the child the time in his day you will return and what you will do together when you return. This reassures him that you really will come back. Also, try to leave him in a comfortable situation in his own home or a familiar setting, with an accepted baby-sitter, relative, or friend.

"One day I stepped out to get something while my daughter was napping, and she was awake before I got back. She raised such a rumpus in the few minutes before I got back that my mother could not console her. Now she clings and won't let me out of her sight. I realize now that I should have told her before she took her nap."

Many parents worry that their child won't nap or go to bed if they know the parent is going out. A child *does* accept a parent's leaving more easily if told when you will return. At worst, the child may lose a little sleep, but she will not lose her sense of trust in the parent.

Bribes and Gifts

"We tell our son that we will bring him something when we return. This makes it easier for him to let us go, but figuring out what to bring home each time is getting to be a problem."

"My sister used that system with her kids and pretty soon they were asking her and everyone who came to visit, 'What did you bring me?' "

That method has many pitfalls. Material gifts may become a substitute for what should be the real emphasis—the return of the parent.

"We have a different problem. My son is used to our leaving in the morning as we both work. He likes his baby-sitter. When we get home he climbs all over us, and it's almost impossible even to get our coats off. I'd like to change clothes, and his father needs to relax a little. But our son wants to engage us in play at once. Is that normal now? Shouldn't he know to wait until we are ready?"

A child this age has no concept of another person's needs. Your child knows only that he has missed you and has been waiting for your return. When you come back, he needs your undivided attention immediately. Of course, you have reasonable needs, too. But if you play with your son first, you can perhaps change your clothes in a more relaxed manner. Daddy may find that playing a few minutes with his son can be relaxing, too. He is tired from doing his work but may have reserve energy to do something different. If he had a gym appointment after work or a tennis game, he would have energy for that.

"I am home all day with our son. When his father comes home, he is all over him before he takes his coat off. Sometimes my husband hardly has time to greet me. At first I was a little annoyed, but I thought it over and decided I could wait to be greeted. But it does take getting used to."

"My child used to behave that way, so my husband worked out a system. He picks our son up, kisses him, kisses me, and then has our son help him get his coat off and walk him to the shower and wait while he showers and changes. Then they play until dinner. Now my son says, 'Shower, daddy, then I play.'"

When children are very young, parents have to do the adjusting. As they grow and mature, they begin to adapt to some of our patterns. This is the stage they are entering now, although some are more advanced than others.

Bedtime Separation

"We don't have a problem leaving our daughter during the day anymore. But at night when we try to put her to bed, she doesn't want to be alone. She wants us to be with her. It doesn't take very long—maybe ten minutes of sitting with her and she's asleep. Why is that still necessary?"

Leaving the warmth of the family and going to bed is a separation. For some children, it is more difficult than other separations. Perhaps it's the fear of waking and not finding the parents there. All these difficulties will disappear as the child matures.

"Our daughter can spend a night at Grandma's without us, but she still needs us to stay with her at a birthday party."

Most children this age can tolerate a parent's leaving a room without following. Some may be able to be left for an hour or two at Grandma's, or at a neighbor's house they have visited frequently with mother. Some may even be able to stay overnight in a familiar place. Most cannot tolerate their parents leaving at night, do not like it, and protest. Some still have difficulty during the day when mother leaves them at home. Some can separate at bedtime easily; others cannot. There's still great variation.

Gender Identity

Children approaching the age of three are not only interested in anatomical differences but are beginning to be aware of themselves as either male or female and are learning how to fit in these roles.

We have talked before about children's questions concerning anatomical differences between their parents. Have you made any further observations about their discoveries? Do you have questions about this issue?

"My son has gone from just pointing to his father's penis when he is in the bath and asking, 'What dat?' to pointing to his own penis and comparing himself with his father. I used to bathe him with my four-and-a-half-year-old daughter, and he began pointing to her genital area as though he thought something was missing. So I just said 'That's your penis' when he pointed to it and 'That's her vagina.' I have stopped bathing them together."

Your son and most children in this age group are establishing their own sexual identity. In a situation such as the one you describe, a parent can say, "You are a boy. You have a penis. Your sister is a girl. She has a vagina." It should be said in a matter-of-fact way that indicates they are of equal importance. This method helps not only in explaining anatomical differences, but in establishing gender identity.

Homosexuality

"Can a boy be born with the tendency to behave more like a girl or a girl with the tendency to behave more like a boy? Can a child be born that way, or is it the result of upbringing?"

There is no absolute answer to that question yet, but there are many theories. Some researchers have evidence that leads to the conclusion that homosexuality is a physiological phenomenon. Most other experts believe that it is a result of childhood experiences.

"There is so much talk about homosexuality now. I've been wondering how much parents influence a child's sexuality and how much is inborn."

Each child is born with hormonal and biochemical differences. That is the child's endowment; it can't be changed. However, the experiences to which the child is exposed, as well as the way parents, relatives, friends, caretakers, and others respond to the child, influence the child's self-image and sexual identity. In addition, each culture has certain standards for the feminine and masculine roles.

"Do you mean that if my son cries, for instance, and we say to him something like 'Be a big boy and don't cry,' we are influencing his sexual identity?"

Yes, the commonly held view is that boys have to be big and strong and not cry, that crying is for babies and females.

"What about girls? If I say to a little girl who is being rough in her play that 'little girls don't do that! Be gentle,' am I influencing her to be gentle?"

Yes. When we make such comments, we are saying that boys can't cry, that it isn't manly, and that only girls are gentle. We are denying that crying is an appropriate expression of sorrow for both boys and girls. Isn't it better to allow boys to cry and girls to be assertive?

"Even now that women are working outside the home and men are helping with child care, I still feel a little uneasy when my son cries over some disappointment. The thought flashes through my mind, 'Will he be a sissy?' "

We are in a transition period. Some of the old views still linger.

"I have no hesitation in letting my daughter play with a truck, but I still feel uneasy when a little boy comes over and gets interested in her dolls, especially when his mother is present and seems to be disturbed by it."

It seems there is a fear that playing with dolls will at best make a "sissy" out of a boy and at worst there is the fear of homosexuality.

"What kinds of childhood experiences do experts think play a role in determining homosexuality?"

Remember that these theories were developed by therapists based on case studies. Some have validity and have been useful in therapy. One of the most frequently heard theories is that a very dominant mother may cause her son to fear or distrust females and seek comfort and affection from males. Another theory is that a very dominant father may cause a son to withdraw from a male identification and prefer female activities.

Other explanations have to do with the "family romance" theory, which holds that the child is sexually attracted to the parent of the opposite sex and, frightened by these feelings, defends himself by continuing to prefer relationships with members of the same sex. Most cases of homosexuality are not so simple, but are associated with more than one cause.

The Family Romance

"We hear so much about the Oedipal complex. Is that what you are referring to as family romance?"

At some time when a child is between three and five, the family romance phenomenon begins. For example, a little girl says, "I'm going to marry Daddy," and if Mommy asks what she should do, the girl says, "You can go away" or "You'll marry the mailman" or "Go and live with your Mommy." A little boy will want his Daddy to go away so that he can take care of Mommy. He wants Mommy to be his girl.

Sigmund Freud found that some people do not get beyond this level of development. For example, a boy may not be able to part from his mother or focus his attention on any other woman. Freud found this in his practice and then related it to the Greek tragedy *Oedipus Rex,* by Sophocles, in which Oedipus unknowingly murdered his own father and then married his own mother. Freud called the situation in which the son's interest remains in the mother the Oedipal complex.

Similarly, a girl may be so attached to her father that she can't form a close attachment to any other male. This is called the Electra complex (again, after Greek legend and a tragedy by Sophocles).

As children grow older and have had good relationships with each parent, they can then attach their affections and attention to other people of the opposite sex. Otherwise the attachment to the parent of the opposite sex may become pathological if a father is consciously or unconsciously seductive to his daughter, or a mother to her son.

Everybody goes through this stage in some form or other for different durations. It's a stage of development during which children are establishing affectional relations. A girl can stay identified with her mother; she does not have to make a change. But a boy has to make a change to identify with his father. This may be difficult—if, for example, the father is stern or not overtly loving.

"Our daughter recently announced, 'When I grow up I'm going to marry Daddy.' I responded, 'No, you will find your own daddy to marry. You will find the man who will be the daddy to your children.' After much thought she said, 'I'm afraid I may not be able to find him.' Her father said, 'We will help you.' We think that families should help their children in making the right marriage."

All parents want to help their children make a right choice. This is not always possible. But they can make it possible for them to have contact with what they feel are desirable members of the opposite sex.

By about age five, the Oedipal stage should be disappearing. But parents should continue to offer alternatives, such as "Yes, you do like Daddy a great deal now, but when you grow up you will find a man who is just as nice."

"Today, girls wear overalls and slacks like boys, and boys have long hair and play with girls' toys. Some fathers perform child care and household chores, while some mothers work and assume some traditionally masculine roles. Aren't sexual distinctions less clear today?"

It is true that clothes and hairstyles, and household roles and outside work roles, are less distinct sexually. But the most important influence on a child's sexual identity is the way the parents relate to each other. This is the model the child will adopt for behavior as a boy or girl and later as a man or woman.

"Do you mean that if my wife and I are always arguing with each other, our child will have the same kind of setup when he or she is grown?"

In most cases, that is so. For example, if a boy's father is always berating his wife, the boy accepts this as the masculine role. He may relate to women in the same way and set up that kind of marriage. If, on the other hand, the wife is always belittling the father, the son may come to believe that males should accept this treatment from females and may later accept that kind of relationship.

Parental Disagreements

"I can understand that we don't want to bring up our daughters as shrews or our sons as tyrants, but what should parents do if and when they have disagreements?"

Disagreements occur in every family. It is important for children to see parents disagree and then resolve the difference. If the relationship between parents is one of basic mutual respect and affection the children have good models to follow, and they are less likely to have confusion in their sexual identity.

■   ■

Coping with Anger

9

The Effect of Anger on Children

Anger is an issue that is of concern throughout our lives. Many people have difficulty dealing with anger appropriately. Parents worry about the effect of their displays of anger on a growing child.

 Now that the children are approaching age three and are experimenting and exploring more, they are more apt to encounter parental disapproval and anger. Parents may expect children to have better judgment than is realistic, and become upset or angry with the child for her exploratory activities or her failure to respond to limitations. Children may respond by becoming submissive, inhibited, fearful, or withdrawn. Others respond with their own anger. Some children defend against anger by ignoring it.

At this age, children are more verbal and better able to understand, so heated encounters between parents can affect them in ways not anticipated by the parents. The interpretation made by the child may be more devastating than arguing parents realize, and can affect the child's behavior and mood. Overhearing parents discussing a difference of opinion in loud voices can make a child very anxious.

When the children were younger, we discussed how parents deal with anger at their children and toward each other. Now that they are getting to be close to age three, how do you feel about this issue?

"I find that I get angry more often with my son now than I used to because he is so active now. Sometimes he cries and begs me not to be angry, and then I feel very guilty for being so severe."

"When my daughter plays with her doll, she yells at it in the same tone that I use. Although it's amusing, it certainly makes me wish I hadn't used that tone."

"It is not so bad when you hear your child imitate you to a doll, but when it's to another child or an adult it sounds just awful. What can be done to cut down on that yelling?"

It is very hard to change a habitual style of responding. In some cases, it may be the result of the example set by your own parents. In others, it is due to fatigue or the pressures of daily life. When parents become conscious of the reasons they respond with anger, they can, with effort and practice, cut down on angry responses. It is part of the growing a parent has to do.

"If something has gone wrong and I am angry about it—even if it is not something my son had done—I get angry and impatient with the least little thing that he does and scold him unnecessarily."

"I don't scold. I am curt. My voice doesn't go up. I try to be in control as far as the children are concerned, but they sense it and get upset."

Anger can be misdirected. It often spills over onto innocent and unsuspecting individuals. Children are likely victims of misdirected anger, because they are always exploring and in need of attention that a parent in a state of suppressed anger is unable to give calmly.

"Yesterday the grocer delivered my order before we got home. A dog, a child, someone had gotten into it and it was strewn in the hall. Of course, I was upset and angry because the delivery boy didn't leave the order with the super, as he was supposed to. My little girl noticed a box of crackers she loves and opened it out in the hall. This was enough to provoke a tirade from me. I know I shouldn't have yelled at her, but I did."

How else do you think you could have handled the situation?

"The sensible thing to do was to open the door and let my daughter into the apartment, let her have her cracker, pick the groceries up and put them into the house, and then call the store and give them my tirade if I still felt angry."

The best way to deal with anger is to confront the one who caused it. However, there may be times when one can't do that. For example, a father has had a bad day at the office because his boss has been unreasonable and demanding. Still upset when he comes home, he opens the door and stumbles over a toy that hasn't been put away. He lets the child have it for every injustice that he has suffered. His anger is out of proportion to the situation and really does not have anything to do with the child.

"What should be done? Something like this must happen in households every day."

A single episode like that does not cause irreparable damage. However, if that kind of encounter is a frequent occurrence, children are affected.

■   ▓

Children of this age are aware of their parents' attitudes and moods. Some withdraw from a parent who is always angry, some respond angrily in any encounter, and others become very inhibited. So anger can have serious repercussions for a child.

If a parent can't change his way of relating to his child by recognizing that he is projecting anger onto his child and trying to relate to the child in a more appropriate way, then the parent should perhaps seek professional help.

"What can a parent do after such an episode if it only happens once in a while?"

The children are now old enough to understand when a parent says she is sorry. The parent can explain that she was upset about something else and didn't mean to be angry with the child (or was tired, or had a headache, or was in a hurry—whatever the reason), then suggest they share an activity that the child enjoys like reading a book, playing ball, or going for a ride.

"But won't apologizing undermine a parent's authority?"

A child approaching the age of three is beginning to be able to understand the concept of an apology—regret for doing something wrong and a promise not to do it again. A parent who can admit a mistake and make amends sets a good example for a child. However, this cannot be exploited, so that the child gets the message that one can make mistakes all the time and all one has to do is apologize. One has to try to emphasize "not doing it again."

"I work outside of the home. With trying to be a mother, too, I guess I'm always in kind of a rush. I get angry when I'm rushing around the kitchen and my son gets underfoot or wants to play. Then I realize that he needs me for that, too, so I feel guilty and apologize."

It is difficult to hold down two jobs, inside and outside of the home. A mother in this situation should attend to important tasks and let others go so that there is time to play with a child. Making that adjustment and feeling comfortable with it can help a mother deal with daily frustrations without anger.

"I've made that adjustment, but sometimes my husband gets upset about the way some chores are neglected. Once in a while we have words about it, which seems to terrify my daughter. She runs to both of us, hugs us, and begs us to 'be nice.' It's never a serious quarrel, just a few loud words, but she stays upset."

"What may happen to a child who is exposed to parents who argue a lot? That's our way of relating to each other. We're both very argumentative."

■   ■

Children of all ages become very upset when parents are angry with each other. Some children immediately feel that they are the cause of the anger; they cling to parents and may develop a fear of being abandoned. Some exhibit sleep disturbances or have appetite changes. Some are irritable and contrary with peers and parents. When a child shows changes in any of these areas, a stress in the family may be the cause.

"Are you saying that parents should never show anger to the child or to each other? That just isn't possible, even in the best of homes."

That is not what we are saying. A child who does something unacceptable has to be told that it is not acceptable—that you are displeased, perhaps even angry. He has to know what makes you angry and what pleases you. One of the parents' jobs is to teach that distinction consistently and patiently.

However, when parents show anger with each other or someone else, children of this age may not be able to cope with it. They may interpret the anger to mean that something awful is going to happen to them. Of course, there are occasional outbursts in any family. Constant exposure to anger can result in personality difficulties which we are trying to prevent or at least minimize. Generally speaking, however, there should be no loud arguments in the presence of children. If parents must argue, they should go out for a walk or argue after the children are sound asleep. The way we express anger is the model that we set for our children. If we always use a loud voice, throw things and slam doors, that is the way our children will express it. If we "clam up" and use the silent treatment and glare at each other, that is what they will do.

"So our example is important, but it's not fatal if they see us angry occasionally?"

That's right. However, you need to let your child know that he is not the cause of the anger. That is important because when children think they are the cause of the anger, they may also think that you will leave them. The fear of abandonment is one of the frequent fears of early childhood and remnants of this fear may persist into adult life.

Resolution of Anger

"Then it's okay to quarrel in front of a child if we make sure he understands he is not the cause?"

That is part of it, but not all. The child should also see a resolution of the quarrel. He needs to see a restoration of normal feelings between the parents—a "kiss and make up" ending, if you will.

■   ■

Physical Violence

"What if the parents come to blows?"

A child must never be a witness to physical violence between parents. For one thing, it is very frightening for the child. The witness to violence is emotionally beaten, too. Your way of showing anger is the model for your child; later in life, this is the way he will behave when angry. This is how family violence becomes sanctioned and perpetuated.

"So the message seems to be that kids can see us angry, but we better mind how we do it. If we don't want generations of fighting mothers and fathers, we'd better kiss and make up."

That about sums it up. We want to teach our children that it is okay to be angry, and demonstrate for them how to express and resolve anger.

Your Child's Anger

We have been discussing your angry feelings and the effects of anger on children. How do you deal with your children when *they* get angry?

"This is a situation that comes up almost every day, and on some days more than once. When my son was an infant, he would cry and get red in the face. I used to think it was funny for a baby to be angry. But when he gets angry now, it's different. It upsets me. All I want him to do is to stop crying and tell me what is bothering him."

"My problem is that whenever my child gets angry, I get frightened. I think she is going to be just like my sister, who is always angry at something. I yell for her to stop, which doesn't help."

It's quite natural to want a child to stop an angry display, whether he is just crying or doing something more physical, like pounding his mother with his fists. We often hear a parent scold and say, "Stop that crying this minute! I can't help you till you stop." This effort to squelch the anger may inhibit the child, and the child may later be unable to express anger appropriately.

"What is a better way to handle such a situation?"

Parents should try to determine what causes an angry response in their child. When the child gets angry, you can say that you know he is upset, but that if he can tell you what is bothering him you will see if you can make the situation better. This way he is given a chance to express his feelings without being scolded, and he is shown that there can be a resolution to the problem.

Supermarket Outbursts

"Sometimes my child throws a tantrum in the middle of the supermarket if I won't buy him something he wants. I get embarrassed and want to wring

his neck, but I control myself and get him out of the supermarket as fast as possible."

If you know that your child is apt to get angry in certain situations, you have several options. Either do not take him to the supermarket or, before you go, tell him what he will be able to have at the market (and get his snack first) and that you will not buy candy or gum. However, if the outburst still ensues, you can pick him up, hold him close and tell him you know he is upset because he wants what he cannot have, but he can have whatever you have agreed upon. He will learn what is expected and the outbursts will diminish, although he may still frequently test you. Parents must remember that a tired child cannot respond reasonably. Very little is effective when the child is tired, except getting the child home and to bed as quickly as possible.

"Both of us work, so on the weekend we try to get most of the week's shopping done. Naturally, we have a lot to buy and we must rush. Our daughter gets upset, because we don't have time to let her pick items off the shelves. Shouldn't she be able to understand that we are in a hurry?"

Children of this age still cannot hurry. As we have said before, their nervous systems just can't process thoughts, sensations, and experiences rapidly. It is better to allow extra time and shop more slowly.

Unsolicited Advice

"Now that my son is almost three, he responds pretty well if I am patient following his angry outbursts. But in a public place there are always people offering advice such as 'What that kid needs is a good spanking,' or 'If he were my kid, I'd give him a whack on the behind and he'd shut up.' "

The important thing is to concern yourself with your child's feelings, not theirs. You don't want to escalate your child's anger by a demonstration of your own.

"I have to confess that at first I get upset and feel hurt when my child gets angry at me. Then I realize that he is a person, too, and has a right to express his feelings. I try to find out what is wrong and to comfort him. He has been responding quite well to that approach."

"Now that my daughter is almost three, she is able to tell me what is making her angry, and it's a little easier to handle her anger now. This morning in the park, she was screaming furiously because she wanted a little boy's fire engine. I told her that she had her doll and that when the boy was finished playing with his fire engine maybe he would give her a turn. She was able to accept that. But it is not always that easy."

■   ■

"I've noticed that when I stop my daughter from doing something or don't give her what she wants right away, she can accept it if I give her the reason. For instance, if she wants to put on a party dress when we are going for a walk, I may say, 'That's a party dress. We are not going to a party. How about wearing the blue dress?' She accepts that explanation. In the past, she would stamp her feet and cry."

Some of you are confirming what we have been trying to point out in all our discussions—that as the children become more mature and are able to say more, they are better able to accept limitations without angry outbursts.

Approval and Disapproval

As the children grow older and become more competent and more venturesome, parents find themselves cautioning and admonishing them more. Parents may fall into the trap of recognizing only the child's misdeeds, neglecting to recognize the child's achievements. Many parents have been brought up by parents who believed that achievements are to be expected and therefore should not be specially recognized. Many children raised this way get the feeling that they can never please their parents and may stop trying. Or they may seek recognition and reassurance constantly.

Are you finding that you spend more time disapproving than approving? Do you think your child is beginning to understand what he is expected to do and what he is not expected to do?

"I don't know if we just are lucky to have a child who responds, but I find we are not always saying 'No.' There are plenty of times our son does things we approve of, and we let him know we are pleased."

I notice that you do not know whether to attribute your child's responsiveness to luck or to something you did. In most cases, it is a combination of both. Each child is different. Some need a good deal of repetition before they internalize and accept a particular limit. All children need overt recognition and approval of acceptable behavior.

Picking Up Toys

"Our clashes now are mostly over picking up toys. Our daughter is better than she used to be, but it still takes a long time for her to come around. If I say, 'When we pick up the toys, then we can go for a walk,' she may start picking them up right away. But usually I have to start and then she joins in."

"We have a similar problem. Sometimes my son says, 'I'm tired, you do it.' I feel like saying, 'You do it this minute,' the way my mother did. Instead, I say, 'We'll do it together. I'll help you.' When it's done I say, 'Look, you

helped and we did a wonderful job.' I feel better, and he looks happy."

"Sometimes that works for us. Once in a while my son absolutely refuses to pick up his toys. I say, 'We'll go to the park when you've picked them up.' If he doesn't do it, we don't go to the park that day. He knows it, so he starts to put them away, although sometimes he waits awhile."

Putting away toys is a big issue at this stage of a child's development. In a few months, when they start nursery school, this will be part of the daily routine, so mothers should be beginning this at home now.

However, we can't expect them to comply every time. You are discovering that your child responds if you are patient. When a child does comply, it is important to offer recognition of the accomplishment. This helps the child feel good about himself and his accomplishment.

"I try to be patient, but I just can't all the time. Some days I yell. Sometimes my daughter gets scared and runs to comfort me. That makes me feel guilty, so I put the toys away and apologize for yelling."

"I yell sometimes, too, but I get nowhere. My son just looks bewildered at me, but he doesn't put his toys away."

An occasional angry outburst is not fatal. Harm comes when this becomes the norm. A child needs parental guidance that is patient, supportive, and approving.

Noisy Play

"What bothers me is rough, noisy play in the house. My son likes to throw his ball in the house and hit things with it. He rides his tricycle up and down the hall, and is delighted when he crashes into something. He builds with his blocks and crashes his buildings so he can start a new one. I'm constantly saying, 'No, don't do that anymore. Stop this minute.' He may stop for a minute, but he goes right back to some other noisy activity."

Many children of this age like to make loud noises and engage in large-muscle activity. It gives them a sense of power and control. However, if the noise upsets you so that you are constantly disapproving of your child's play, you have to set limits. The child should be told that balls and tricycles are for outside. When he plays with his blocks and he takes the structure down without crashing it, you can show him how pleased you are when he does it that way. Then you can encourage indoor play with appropriate toys, like coloring books, puzzles, small cars, and trains. Many children are happy indoors if they are permitted to help with simple chores.

"We've been talking about a child's need for approval. My parents say that if a child is always shown approval at home, he won't be able to cope with

disapproval later in life. They admit that that is why they were so strict with us, and that's the way their parents were with them."

We are not saying that a child has to be shown approval constantly, but that attention should be given to things that are acceptable and deserve approval. Recognition of achievements, however small, helps a child acquire a positive self-image. Many parents overlook achievements because they expect them from the child.

10

Fathers' Expectations

Both a father's involvement and his expectations are very important, because his role is a model for both daughters and sons. Fathers, like mothers, have concerns and expectations that should be addressed.

The children are now approximately three. I've met with many of you fathers before to discuss the issues of development. Are there any issues that you would like to discuss now?

Stages of Conversation

"How should I respond when my son is very demanding and commands me to do something? My instinct is to get angry and tell him he can't talk like that. Am I too hard with him?"

The commanding tone is part of the child's language development. Normal conversation comes later. Remember how they repeated their first words? They learned how to name objects. After that they put words together in phrases, then in sentences. They announced their observations, then they commanded.

"I think that's what makes it difficult, because sometimes we can talk very nicely together, then suddenly they go into these commands."

Usually this regression occurs when they are tired.

"Yes, that's right, at night."

When they are tired, they fall back to a stage you think is over. By that time you are tired, too, because it's the end of the day, so that makes it even more difficult.

"Yes, I can see that. It kind of sums up the situation. I guess it will just take a little more time and I don't need to get angry and offended by his tone."

"I have the same situation and its upsets me. I really feel hurt because I expected something different in the way of communication. I am upset when I take off a weekend to be with my son

and he is so demanding. It's good to know this isn't going to be the way he will behave all the time."

This is usually a passing phase. Most children go through it successfully if the parents don't take offense and answer in disagreeable tones.

Interrupting Conversations

"Is it too much to expect children to keep quiet and let adults talk? I can't remember when I've been able to talk to my wife without being interrupted by our son. I love my son but still I have needs, too."

"Our son, is the same way. I could understand that he needed constant attention as an infant, but now he is going on three."

Children need to feel included. They cannot understand that parents may have to discuss matters that are not the child's concern. For children this age it is best to pick them up and hold them and say, for example, "Daddy is telling Mommy about what happened in the office today." The child may then wiggle away to play on his own for a few minutes, giving you a moment to talk. More lengthy, discussions can be conducted after the child is asleep or when you are out together without your child.

"When we are in the car, our son doesn't let us converse unless we include him. If we try to talk only to each other, he says, 'Stop talking so much.' "

That behavior is characteristic of children this age. They interrupt because they cannot accept exclusion. If you have to discuss something that isn't related to the child, save if for when the child is not there.

"You just can't expect it? We have told him that Mommy and Daddy have to talk, and that he can watch the cars go by while we are talking."

You can say, "Watch and see if there is a yellow car. Tell me when you see one." Then you do a *little* talking until he interrupts.

They are at a stage when they can delay a little. For instance, if you are finishing a sentence with your wife, you can say "Just a minute dear" and finish the sentence and then turn your attention to the child. This, of course, may not lead to smooth conversation.

Parental Disappointment

"I like athletics, and I always thought we would play ball together— baseball or basketball. When I go out to play on Saturday, I take him to watch me. But he isn't interested. He sits in his carriage and calls for me, or if I let him he runs in the way of the ball."

You are expecting something of him for which he is too young. At this stage of his development, you might be able to get him interested in playing ball if you just throw a light ball to him in a park or yard. He may not be able to catch it, but he may be able to learn to throw to you. At least you'll be playing together regularly.

"My wife and I both work. On the weekends my wife has lots of chores, so I thought I'd be biking with my daughter on Saturday mornings and give my wife some time on her own. Our child manages a kiddle car well, but she is nowhere near ready to pedal even a tricycle. So I take her out in her carriage and long for the time we'll be able to bike."

Some parents purchase child seats which sit on the adult bikes, either behind or in front. You may enjoy riding with your child in that way in a safe place.

Bedtime

"If our daughter went to bed earlier, we'd have more time for each other. I think my wife has been too lenient and lets her stay up too long."

Each family has its own daily routine. In some families fathers come home early, so the child gets used to an early bedtime. In other families, the routine is different; perhaps the father comes home later, so the child's bedtime is later. If both parents work, the evening is the only time they can be with the child, so the child's bedtime may be quite late.

"I think one of the reasons our son won't go to sleep till quite late is that he has a nap around four-thirty. When he gets up, about five-thirty or six, he is rested and ready to go until nine or ten. I think he could skip his nap and go to bed earlier, but my wife says he gets so cranky that he just falls apart."

There may be other solutions. Perhaps coming indoors earlier from the afternoon's activities and having an earlier and shorter nap would enable him to go to bed earlier. Or perhaps if he came in earlier and had quiet play times, then an early bath and supper, he would be ready to be put to bed by you when you come home. You could institute bedtime rituals, such as tooth brushing, storytelling, or reading while your wife prepares dinner for the two of you. That would give you time with your child and also time alone with your wife.

"We both work, and we both get home about the same time. Some nights my wife puts our child to bed, I fix the food, and we all eat together. The next night we swap chores. The one who cooked the food puts the baby to bed and the other cleans up."

"I don't see why that arrangement couldn't work for us, too. Even though my wife is home, our child is so active that he takes so much out of her and she can use help with dinner. I know because he wears me out, too, if I'm with him all day."

"For me some of the fun is being taken out of it because of the way our child behaves. She seems to have a mind of her own. I think it's because my wife is too lenient. She thinks I'm too strict and expect too much. Is it too much to expect our daughter to come home from an outing without putting up a fuss and crying?"

It is normal for children this age to have difficulty moving from one activity to another. Adults have to remember that children's activities are as important to them as our activities are to us. We don't like interruptions either. We don't like to be stopped in the middle of a tennis game or a party or while working on a project to do something that we haven't been warned or consulted about. Children feel the same way. Their way of dealing with it is to cry, ours is to discuss it and come to some resolution.

"Does that mean we should just give in to them?"

Certainly not. There are better ways to approach the problem. One way is to give the child warning: "In a few minutes it will be time to go home." Then say "it is time" and get the child ready for the next activity. There will still be some protest. The parent can say "I know you would like to stay but now it's time for [whatever]. We'll be back another day" and continue getting the child ready. Another way is by letting the child know what awaits him. "We are going home to supper and we are going to have your favorite————" or "We will stop to look at the fish in the window at the pet shop."

"But what if they protest anyway?"

They will protest at first, but if they feel that you are calm, confident, and not ambivalent, and that you know what you are doing, they will respond after a few experiences of this kind of treatment.

The fathers have all expressed reasonable expectations. The important thing is to keep the child's level of development in mind and then be consistent without being angry in helping the child achieve the desired response.

Manners

Each culture has its own standards of behavior. Most parents want their children to have good manners and they may have their own personal reasons for such concerns. We discussed manners before, but some of your expectations were a little ahead of your children's abilities. How are you dealing with this issue now?

"Our child has begun to use his spoon and fork more regularly. We let him know that we are pleased when he uses his utensils properly. He smiles and nods his head. I think he tries a little harder."

"We're seeing progress too, especially with the spoon, now that our son has the hang of it. But he sometimes shoves too much into his mouth at once and we have to remove the excess."

Many of you are witnessing improved and more consistent use of the spoon and fork. With practice and positive recognition from parents, the

■   ■

children's dexterity will continue to increase. Sometimes they still use their hands, and many children fill their mouths too full at times and have be to shown how much to take.

It's a good idea to have them watch while you eat. Show them exactly how much you put on a spoon or fork, how you chew with your mouth closed, and then swallow before taking the next bite. Then watch the child do it and acknowledge success.

"My spontaneous response is 'No, not that way.' I raise my voice, and I guess I'm a little scary, because my daughter begins to cry and the whole meal is ruined."

Scolding doesn't help matters. Your daughter and most other children learn best when the correct way is modeled for them and their efforts to follow your example are recognized.

"We are making some progress with 'please' and 'thank you,' but there are many lapses. How much should we expect at this stage?"

They may not always remember to say "please" and "thank you." When they do lapse, a gentle reminder is useful.

"You mean if my child asks for a cookie, I should say, 'When you say, "please," I'll give you a cookie'?"

There are several ways to get your point across without being angry or harsh. You can say, in a pleasant tone "When you say please I'll be glad to give you a cookie," or "I think you mean 'Please may I have a cookie.' " Most children respond to this approach.

"If he refuses to say 'please,' should I give him the cookie anyway?"

The first time it happens on any given day, try saying something like "I guess you forgot to say 'please.' Try to remember it next time." The next time, you can say in a pleasant way, "How are we supposed to ask?" or "What is the magic word?" Show approval when he complies, so that his self-esteem is bolstered and he can see that compliance brought emotional rewards.

"My son does fine with 'please' and 'thank you'—except when Grandma comes, when I want him to be especially nice. I get a little edgy when that happens."

We always want our children to behave well when we have company. Now that the children are almost three and are able to understand and say so much more, we expect them to perform well as social beings. If this anxiety is conveyed to the child, the child may become anxious, too, and forget some of the things he has learned. Try saying, "I guess we forgot to say 'please.' Let's try to remember it for next time." In that way you let the visitor know you are aware of the lapse. At the same time, you do not embarrass your child and set up a tense situation for the next time company comes.

"What about saying 'hello' and 'good-bye' now? When we talked about it last time, you told us to say it for them and set the example."

"My daughter still hides behind me and still can't say 'good-bye.' She is a little better at 'hello' and 'hi.' "

For some reason, most children have more difficulty with greetings and partings than with "please" and "thank you." Some children may not accomplish this until they are four or five, and may need to be reminded even at that age.

"So we shouldn't force the issue?"

That's right. Set an example for the child. Give the other person and the child the feeling that he is included by saying "hello" and "good-bye." Before the visit, you can remind the child of the appropriate things to say. You can say, for instance, "We are going to visit Grandma. Let's remember to say, 'Hello, Grandma.' And when we leave, let's remember to say, 'Good-bye, Grandma.' " That sometimes may help.

"When visitors come, we still can't carry on an uninterrupted conversation. Before we were married and had children, that used to annoy me so much that I vowed I'd never let my children do it."

At three years of age, children may find it difficult to be excluded. They simply can't understand why a parent is unavailable to them when a visitor comes. But if you make an attempt to include the children in your conversation, they are more likely to leave you alone and continue with their own play. They may still interrupt, but they may be able to wait until you finish a sentence.

"Our child still doesn't sit through a whole meal; she has to get up and run around. That's okay at home, but not in a restaurant. And we do like to eat out once in a while."

A child this age who can sit through a meal is still the exception. Most children of this age can't be expected to sit through more than about twenty minutes of a meal. By that time they have usually finished all that they are going to eat anyway. They are still not ready to go to a restaurant where service takes time and where an active or young child is not welcome. As they get older, they learn to sit longer at the table.

"Our daughter recently sat through a full-course holiday dinner at a family gathering. We were very proud. But she doesn't do that every day at home, and we accept that. We tell her that when she is a big girl she'll be able to sit at the table and talk with Daddy and Mommy. Is that right?"

That is right. You are simply letting her know what her goals should be, and that what she does now is acceptable.

Unacceptable Language

"Our son regularly goes to the park, where some of the children are older. He comes back with a few words we don't use at home. I don't know where those children pick up this vocabulary, but it's shocking. Should we explain why we don't want him to use these words?"

At this age he isn't likely to understand your explanation. You can simply tell him that you don't like those words and that you don't use them. If there are appropriate substitutes for the words, supply them. If he continues to use the words calmly restate your position and then be unresponsive when he uses them. The words will probably disappear from his vocabulary from lack of reinforcement.

"My son said 'shut up' to me the other day. I was so shocked that I laughed, so he repeated it."

If you laugh when a child does something surprising or cute for this age, the child may try to evoke that response again. It may take time for him to then accept no response and to stop.

Sharing

"What about sharing? Last week, we had friends over. They brought their son, who is almost four. For the first half hour, my son made a fuss every time this boy touched a toy of his. We gave them some snacks and after that it was much better, but we were a little embarrassed."

The children's ability to share is still erratic. They are better able to share with children they know and see often. In nursery school next year, they will learn to take turns and to share. They will also be more verbal and better able to negotiate with other children. Now, however, they still need to be reassured that a visiting child will only play with a toy and not take it home.

Shopping

"When we go into a store, my child touches objects that she shouldn't. Once she squeezed an egg and broke it. I'm trying to get her to understand that she must ask me first if she may touch an object."

"I can't go into a toy store with my son without holding on to him, because he gets into everything. I've stopped taking him to stores."

Children this age are curious and constantly want to touch and explore. It is very difficult for them to understand that it is wrong to touch something that is very tempting. Parents should try to steer clear of such temptations whenever possible until the children are a little older and their self-control is stronger. If parents are patient, they can teach children the concept that certain things are off limits—Mommy's perfume and lipstick, for example.

They can be told that certain things belong to other people and are not to be touched without asking.

Weaning

One important indicator of development is the ability to relinquish the bottle. Most of the children have been drinking from a cup successfully for several months. Many children have already given up the bottle, although some still need the first morning and the last evening bottle. Are any of you concerned about your children's progress with weaning?

"My son still needs a morning and evening bottle, and I've been wondering just when and how I should go about getting him to give them up."

Although most children give up the bottle around three, three is not a magical number. Some children are ready earlier than age three; others need a little longer. By this time most of their milk consumption should be from a cup, even if assistance is necessary. A child may give up the night bottle more easily if she is held on mother's lap while drinking the last cup of milk. This simulates the position and security of an earlier stage.

"We've been continually reminded that any changes in the child's routine should be in keeping with the child's own readiness timetable. Is encouraging the child to get rid of the bottle consistent with that principle?"

Under no circumstances should a parent take the bottle away abruptly. It should be done in a way that helps the child accept the cup without feeling that he is being separated from a source of comfort. In addition, the child should be given extra attention and recognition for his accomplishment. The parent's job is to help children move to a more mature stage when they are ready.

"My daughter was slow in reaching all her developmental milestones, and I'm not expecting her to be any different with this one. I think I understand her timetable now, and I am comfortable with it, even though I get flak from family."

It can be difficult to cope with the opinions of people who are not with a child all the time and may not be aware of her readiness. You can remind these people that every child has his or her own maturational timetable and that you certainly intend to stop the late-evening bottle as soon as you feel your daughter is ready.

"I went through that with my mother. Finally I said, 'Mom, I assure you he will not be having a bottle when he goes to college, so don't worry.' That worked for me, and maybe it will work for others, too."

"I have a different concern: My son isn't a very good eater. He drinks from a cup quite well, but he doesn't get as much as he does from a bottle. So I'm very glad he takes the late-night bottle."

■   ■

What does your doctor say about your son's health and nourishment? Does he think he requires the night bottle?

"He told me months ago to give it up, that he was fine."

Your anxiety may be making you continue with the last bottle, not your son's readiness. You have to make up your mind when you are ready to try giving him a cup before bedtime.

"My son has given up the night bottle, but not the early-morning one. It's probably my fault. He wakes up so early that I give him a bottle to get him back to sleep for another hour, so that I can sleep a little longer, too! Is that so terrible?"

There is nothing wrong with that if it suits your life-style. Allowing bottles until a child is ready to be weaned and doing it gradually in keeping with the child's readiness is a more appropriate way. We are just discussing ways to relinquish the last bottle.

"What about telling a child that the bottle broke and you have no more, or you lost it?"

"I tried that with my child, and she said, 'Go store bottle'!"

It is never a good idea to tell a child an untruth. Children understand more than we think, and if they sense deceit, it makes them lose trust in what you tell them.

"Last weekend we stayed at a friend's overnight. In the hurry of packing, I forgot my son's bottle. When I put him to bed, I said, 'Mommy forgot your bottle, but you can have a cup of milk like a big boy.' He accepted the cup and went to sleep without a protest. I was sure he'd want the bottle when we got back home, but he hasn't asked for one."

"We recently had overnight guests. We put their daughter on the sofa in our daughter's room. The guest's child had a cup of milk before bed, so I asked our daughter if she would like one. She agreed, and has asked for a cup ever since. She had been so attached to her night bottle—or so I thought— that I was afraid to suggest a cup."

In each case there were two factors that led to success—a situation that presented itself at a time when the child was ready, and a mother who was able to seize the opportunity.

"Maybe I'm the one holding on. My daughter takes a few sips and then drops the bottle or gives it back to me. But I'm afraid to stop offering it to her."

It sounds as though she is trying to tell you she doesn't need the bottle anymore. She might be content with just a sip of water from a cup as part of the bedtime routine.

"My son doesn't drink from a bottle anymore, but he wants to carry one around. Sometimes he keeps the nipple in his mouth for a while and chews on it, but he never seems to suck at it."

■   ■

He is using the bottle as a transitional object. Perhaps in time he will choose a different object.

"We went through that, too. So I said, 'We won't take it outside, just in the house.' My child accepted that, and soon latched on to a truck, which he carries everywhere now."

"What about pacifiers? Don't children have to be weaned from them too?"

A pacifier satisfies the sucking needs of a child who may take bottles too quickly. It is unwise to offer a pacifier as a substitute for the bottle. The child may continue to use it as a means of comfort when it is no longer appropriate.

"What if he does continue to use it all the time? I've seen some children of three and even four who always seem to be sucking on their pacifiers."

Some children seek the comfort of a pacifier when they are anxious, tired, lonesome, or bored. Others use it as a transitional object, much as they become attached to teddy bears, for example. The parent should observe the child and try to correct those situations that cause the child to seek the comfort of the pacifier. For example, if the child is lonesome or bored, a more interesting or stimulating environment should be provided.

"My son gave up the pacifier months ago. But recently we visited friends whose child was using a pacifier. When we got home, he found his pacifier in a box of toys and began to use it, but he didn't keep it up because the rubber was a little stiff and I guess it didn't fill a need."

"I have noticed that when I have my child with me instead of at the baby-sitter's she doesn't use her pacifier. She is an only child, and we are always doing something together at home. But at the baby-sitter's she is one of four children, and she doesn't get all the attention she needs. I understand that, so I try to create a different environment for her at home."

Parents should try to eliminate use of the pacifier without giving the child the feeling that what he is doing is wrong. Perhaps the child can be kept occupied with a more satisfying or constructive activity. This may take consistent effort on the parents' part, like playing more with him, getting him involved in more household chores, and giving him a sense of achievement.

Toilet Training

As the children grow, parents feel increasing pressure to toilet train. Some parents are made to feel as though the speed with which they toilet train the child is a measure of their qualifications as parents. There is also the temptation to compare a child's achievement in this area with that of a neighbor's or friend's child. In addition, many nursery schools require that all children be toilet trained.

■   ■

Some children have achieved bowel and bladder control by this age; others are in various stages of accomplishing this step. How are your children doing in this area?

Readiness for Toilet Training

"My son knows where things go and helps to put them away. He tells me when he has soiled or wet himself and wants to be changed. He seems to understand what we use the toilet for, and what the little seat in the bathroom is for, because he puts his teddy bear on it. He just doesn't connect it with himself yet. Is there anything I can do to encourage him?"

It sounds as though your son is almost ready to be toilet trained. When he puts his teddy bear on the seat, perhaps you can simply point out that someday he is going to be big enough to use the toilet too.

"Mine is entirely oblivious of the issue. I know there is no use forcing him to sit on the toilet. I did that with my first child, and it was a battle all the time. I would not go through that again, because I feel we developed some unpleasant attitudes toward each other that are present to some extent even today."

The anger and resistance a child feels during toilet training can indeed linger. We are trying to avoid such an "angry alliance" between parent and child. It takes patience and understanding on the parents' side to avoid this trap.

"My mother thinks a little clear suggestion doesn't hurt. The other day, after she had been baby-sitting and had to change a soiled diaper, she said to my daughter, 'You are a big girl now, so you can use the toilet the way big girls do.' My daughter looked at her, shook her head, and said, 'Me not big, me little.' "

Children of this age can be quite astute. They have more of a sense of themselves than we give them credit for. They know when they are ready to move ahead, then they have a natural urge to do so.

"My daughter has been using the bathroom successfully for almost two months. She simply announced one day that she wanted to use the toilet, pulled off her Pamper, and pulled me to the bathroom to put her on the potty chair. Now she manages it herself, although she calls me to help her get dressed again. I didn't believe it could happen so easily."

"My daughter asked to use the toilet last week after watching a cousin who had come to visit, and she has been using the toilet since then."

Did she just use it without any help from you? What did she do before that?

"For a few days before that she would ask us to use the toilet. She was rarely successful with urinating, although more often with bowel move-

■   ■

ments. I praised her when she was successful and said nothing when she wasn't. Then, after her cousin's visit, she seemed to be trained."

"My son bypassed the potty chair and insisted on being lifted to the regular toilet seat. I was afraid he would fall in, but he carefully braces himself on his hands and holds himself up. That's for bowel movements. He steps to the toilet and urinates standing up. That came first, after watching his father."

These are success stories that should encourage everyone. Children let their parents know when they are ready.

"I noticed that my daughter was waking dry from her nap, so I suggested that she try to use the bathroom before getting dressed. She accepted the idea and was successful, and since then she has been responding when it is suggested."

Accidents

"My daughter seemed to train herself. When she is left on her own, she doesn't have accidents. But if I want her to use the bathroom before we go out, she balks. Then, once we are outside, she may announce that she needs to use the bathroom. If we are near one we manage, but if not, she may wet herself a little. Is there any way to overcome this?"

She's trying to control herself. Perhaps if you model going to the bathroom as all "big" girls do, she may want to use it, too, when not coerced.

"My daughter can't seem to use an unfamiliar bathroom, so we have accidents when she won't use the bathroom at home before we leave. I was wondering if I should put her back in diapers whenever we go out."

That may confuse your child. She may find it difficult to know when to exert control and when she can revert to an earlier level. The best approach is to leave the house with a change of clean clothes so that the child can be changed if necessary.

"What can you say to a child when he has an accident? When this happens, my son acts as though he has committed a crime and expects me to do something terrible to him."

Each child responds differently to such incidents. Much depends on the child's temperament, how much he wants to win your approval, and what he believes will be the retribution for his failure. The best approach is to be as calm and casual as possible, then say something reassuring, like "It was just an accident. I know you did your best. I brought some clean clothes, and we will change into them as soon as we can."

"Once a child is toilet trained, is it a good idea to take her to the bathroom before going out, so an accident is less apt to happen?"

"I tried that, and I think it caused more problems. Now when I ask my son to use the bathroom before we go out, he insists that he doesn't have to. He

runs away and can't go even if I do take him. Now I just take a change of pants with us."

Sometimes a better approach is to prepare the child by saying, "In a little while, or in five minutes, it will be time for the bathroom." Of course, this works especially well if the child is accustomed to respond to "It is time for dinner [or a bath, etc]." For others it may work better to say, "When you finish your block house [or bathing your doll], it will be time to go to the bathroom."

"I use that method, and usually it works. But once in a while my child just can't make herself go. Then, when we are outside, she has an accident."

When this happens, try not to be angry or lose your temper. Instead, say in a quiet voice, "Maybe if we used the bathroom before going out this wouldn't happen. Let's try next time." This approach usually works better than lecturing the children in a threatening tone.

"Does it make any difference if a child is toilet trained first for bowel movements, then for urinating?"

That depends on the individual child. Sometimes bowel control is accomplished first because bowel movements are less frequent than urination. Some boys achieve urination control first because their anatomy makes urinating a less complicated procedure. In most cases, both types of control are achieved at once if children are allowed to respond on their own timetable.

Fears of Flushing

"My son responded early to bladder training, but he refuses to have a bowel movement on the toilet. So I let him do it in his diaper. When he is ready, he asks me to put his diaper on him. So I do."

"My daughter watched me empty her diaper into the toilet and then flush it away. She asked me where it went, and I explained that it went into the sewer and out to the sea. That frightened her, and she would not let me empty her diaper after that. I had to do it when she was asleep."

This is not uncommon. Some children feel that their bowel movement is part of them and are afraid to have it flushed away. They may fear that they may be flushed away, too.

Night Wetting

"My son is completely trained during the day. When should we expect him to be dry at night, too?"

"What if I pick up my son before I go to bed and take him to the bathroom? Will that help him keep dry?"

Most children this age achieve nighttime control on their own. Those who wet generally do so shortly after falling asleep, perhaps because they are too tired or tense to empty their bladders at bedtime. Parents can help these children achieve nighttime control by awakening them and taking them to the toilet. Other children wet early in the morning, because they wake up before the parents do. These children are usually helped when the parents rise early enough to take them to the bathroom before they wet.

Accidents at Nursey School

"I have been thinking of nursery school next year. Although most of the schools require children to be toilet trained, they also ask that several changes of clothes be left in case of accidents. Are accidents to be expected?"

Accidents do occur frequently. The child who has an accident may have been hurried at home and resisted using the bathroom. However, nursery-school teachers have to be prepared for these accidents. Some children get so engrossed in play that they resist going to the bathroom until it's too late. Many teachers are aware of this and set up regular bathroom times. But accidents continue to happen until the children achieve control. Some children do not achieve full control until they are five or six years old.

"I guess we have to remember that they are still babies even if they are three."

That is something parents are inclined to forget, especially if the child is verbal and bright. The children have made much progress since we last discussed toilet training, and most of them will have good control of bowel and bladder functions by age three or shortly thereafter.

Independence: Learning to Help Themselves

We have discussed weaning children from the bottle and pacifier. Other issues can be approached in the same way. For example, the children should be encouraged to do things for themselves, such as dressing, eating and putting away toys. This helps them experience a gradual increase in delay of gratification. Another is helping them experience the sequence of events that lead to a specific conclusion, so that they can finally accept consequences. They are able to do this as their capacity for language increases and concept formation develops. Are you seeing that the children are trying to take care of some of their needs by themselves? How do you respond?

"I've noticed that my son tries to dress himself. He can get on his shirt and his underpants. But sometimes he does it backward. I let him do it anyway, because he seems so pleased with himself."

"My son tries that too, but he is slow and I have work to do, so I just dress him. It's faster and easier for me."

Children this age should be given a chance to dress themselves. Success enhances their sense of themselves as achievers. Mothers who work outside the home may need to start at an earlier hour to accommodate the child's level of ability in dressing. Each family should decide what works best for them.

"I don't work outside the home, but I can't stand waiting while my daughter gets herself dressed. I just don't have the patience."

As we've said many times before, patience is something parents need to cultivate. It's an important ingredient in many situations, but particularly so in parenting.

"I envy all parents whose children try to do things on their own. Whenever I suggest to my child that she can dress herself, she says, 'No, you, Mommy.'"

Your child may not be quite ready to try on her own, and your urging threatens her. By the time children reach nursery school, at about three, most show an interest in dressing themselves. At nursery school, teachers may show them ways of helping themselves into their outer clothes.

"My child has been eating by herself for quite a while. Although she is sometimes messy and resorts to using her hands to get the food into her mouth, I don't interfere. But when she insists on trying to pour juice or milk she usually spills some. When should children be allowed to pour?"

Most children love to pour. When they were younger they may have been allowed to practice pouring in the bathtub. Now that most of them have better coordination, they can be allowed to pour from a small pitcher to help water plants or to pour a little milk into a cup. Of course, there may be spills. They should not be emphasized. But the successes should be recognized.

Delaying Gratification

"What I'm having a problem with is my son's impatience. He wants everything 'this minute.'"

"My daughter used to be that way, but she is getting to be more patient. I say, 'Just a minute' and then do whatever it is she wants. She is more able to wait—not a long time, but enough so I don't feel as pressured."

Children of this age are beginning to be able to wait a little longer to have their requests satisfied. If parents have been consistent and reliable, a child develops a feeling of basic trust. Since he knows that his parents will see to his needs, he gradually becomes able to wait longer.

"My son is getting pretty good about waiting for things—except going out. I usually have things to do around the house before we go out, but he just can't wait. It becomes like a tug-of-war."

One of the ways to deal with impatient children is to involve them in what you are doing. You can ask your child to help you make the bed, dust, or anything else, so that you will be able to get out faster. Children learn quickly the order of events that lead up to a pleasurable activity.

"I have my son do things for his toy animals—feed them, put them to bed, tell them a story. This cuts down on any pressure that I may feel."

Putting Things Away

"Is it too soon to expect children to put away toys? My daughter's toys are strewn all over by the end of the day."

When children go to nursery school, one of their activities is "putting away time." They get a certain pride in doing it because of the teacher's approval and manner of sharing in the activity. But they can also begin to learn at home now.

"I don't allow my son to take out a new set of toys until we put the first group away, so most of the time we don't have such a big mess. My parents think I'm too strict about it."

Parents all have their own way of dealing with this matter. A child can learn readily if parents are firm and offer recognition of approval when the task is done. Other parents prefer a single clean-up, with cooperation from the child.

Breaking Toys

"When is a child old enough to understand that if he breaks a toy, it may not be possible to repair it?"

A child of this age may not be able to understand cause and effect in this context. If she breaks a toy, she can be shown the damage that is the result of her action. She can be given a simple explanation as well—"When you pull the wheels off your toy car, the car won't go anymore," for example. She may remember this lesson the next time she is playing.

"When my child breaks a toy, he gets extremely upset. If I can't repair it right away, I promise him I will buy him another one. This calms him down, but is it the right thing to do?"

This is a difficult part of parenting, but a very essential one. Children learn to help themselves and to delay gratification if they understand that their actions have consequences. Replacing the toy immediately does not help him learn the consequences.

■   ■

A child who is verbal may be able to understand the consequences of certain actions. A parent is the best judge of when a child is able to comprehend this concept, and should be prepared to help the child learn it at the appropriate time.

Holidays

Most parents remember the things they enjoyed about holidays when they were children or how they wished they had celebrated them and want to impart tradition to their children. However, children at this age may not be prepared for everything that holidays entail. For example, at Halloween they may enjoy the treats but be frightened by masks, costumes, and jack-o'-lanterns. At Christmastime they may enjoy the tree and its bright lights but be frightened by a large and jovial Santa Claus who takes a child on his lap in a store and greets him too heartily.

How have your children been reacting to holiday festivities? How have you been responding to their excitement and tears?

Halloween

"This will be the third Halloween for my son. Last year he was frightened by the masks on kids who came for trick-or-treat. He had trouble getting to sleep that night and for a few nights after that. How much do you think he will understand this year?"

Children younger than three can grasp neither the religious significance nor the fantasy associated with a holiday. However, parents can prepare a child for certain holiday occurrences. On Halloween, for example, the child can be told that there will be visitors in masks and costumes to whom he will give a treat.

"Last Halloween we made a small jack-o-lantern. Our daughter was thrilled and asked us to turn out the lights over and over again so she could see it in the dark. It became a game, and she wasn't upset when children came around with lighted pumpkins. But she was excited and had a hard time getting to sleep that night."

Even something pleasurable can upset a child's sleep routine. Allowing the child a longer time to relax before going to bed usually helps him or her overcome the excitement.

Christmas

"Last year I didn't take my daughter near the department-store Santas. She just watched from a distance. I could tell she was interested, but I didn't think she was ready. I felt she may have been too frightened by the experience. I wonder if it would be fun for her this year."

Christmas can have frightening and fun aspects for children this age. For example, being held by a large and unusually dressed individual in a

■   ■

strange place may be more frightening than pleasant. Most of the children are not yet able to grasp the meaning of Santa Clause anyway. Many parents recall fondly their own childhood Christmasses and are anxious for their children to have similar joyful experiences. But parents must first make certain that their children are ready for the holiday event or activity.

"Should parents tell children they'll get presents only if they behave? I remember the agony I went through caused by threats from my mother and father: 'If you want Santa to bring you that doll, you'd better remember how to behave.' That still rings in my ears around Christmastime."

A child this age can be made anxious by the repeated threat of not being visited by Santa. This method is not in keeping with our view of the correct way to teach discipline: to recognize approved behavior, set limits on disapproved behavior, offer appropriate recognition, and refrain from using threats and bribes.

Anticipation

"My child gets so excited in anticipation of holidays that I try not to say anything until the day before. But preparations for Christmas begin so far in advance that I just can't use that method at Christmastime."

"Christmas is a big event in our family. We all exchange presents. We all bake cookies and make special foods for the big family feast. We try to soft-pedal talk of presents, so as not to get the children overexcited. Still, I hope this year my son will understand more and enjoy the season, if he is a little too excited."

It is hard to make preparations for a big holiday without getting young children excited and anxious. Children this age cannot understand that all these activities are leading to a happy event. Nor are they able to postpone gratification for very long. Children respond differently in this situation. Some become irritable, others have difficulty sleeping or experience loss of appetite. Parents should keep to usual routines as much as possible, and keep festivities as simple as possible.

Disillusionment

"We are troubled by the prospect of having to disillusion our child about Santa Claus. I remember how upset I was when I found out my parents put the presents under the tree. I felt terribly cheated and deceived."

Each family has to decide for itself how to present holiday rituals to the children. Remember, however, that most children of this age don't comprehend the concept of Santa Claus, so disillusionment should not be a concern yet. However, at this age they can enjoy the bright lights of a tree, the presents (whose wrappings may be more enjoyable than the contents), some of the special holiday foods, and the music.

Different Cultures and Customs

"We are members of the Pentecostal Church. We do not tell our children about Santa Claus. Nor do we give gifts on Christmas. It is a religious occasion."

"We, too, do not celebrate Christmas with a tree and Santa Claus. We have a piñata, which is full of small presents. On Christmas we crack it, and all the presents come out. The children enjoy that."

"We are Jewish. Our holiday is Hanukkah, the festival of lights, which comes around the same time of year as Christmas and lasts eight days. Our custom is to give children a small present each night, although some families give only one large present the first night. Our children know the presents are from their parents and grandparents, but there is still a lot of excitement and preparation."

"In a community like ours, where Christmas with Santa Claus is the dominant custom, it is very hard to tell your child that he can't share in the fun because his family doesn't believe in that. So we celebrate our traditions and Santa Claus. That works for us."

Try not to emphasize what the child can't do. Emphasize what he does instead—such as breaking a piñata or exchanging Hanukkah presents. This helps the child establish cultural identity, and to see that having different traditions and beliefs is not bad. Children should be encouraged to learn to understand and enjoy the rituals of people of different religions.

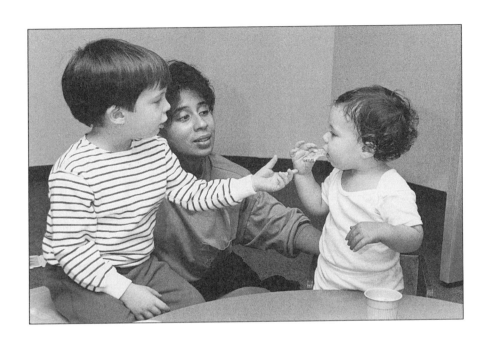

11

New Experiences and Interests

We have been discussing the relationship of parents and children in their immediate families and occasionally in relation to a neighbor or friend. The children are now beginning to take more interest in the world around them—that is, they observe people and what they do and the relationships between people. They want to know who does what and who relates to whom, as well as the function of many inanimate things like trains, cars, and planes. Have you been aware of your child's interest in things outside himself?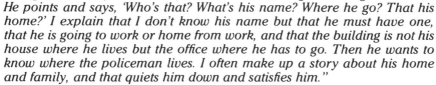

"I find that I take my son more places with me and that he wants to know who people are and what they do. We pass a police station on our way to the supermarket. If it is time for a shift change, there may be several police officers entering or leaving. He points and says, 'Who's that? What's his name? Where he go? That his home?' I explain that I don't know his name but that he must have one, that he is going to work or home from work, and that the building is not his house where he lives but the office where he has to go. Then he wants to know where the policeman lives. I often make up a story about his home and family, and that quiets him down and satisfies him."

That seems to be the answer he wants and needs. He seems to need to place this person in uniform, which he doesn't quite understand, in a context of home and family, which he can understand.

"We went through something similar with my son. Whenever he saw a fire truck go by with sirens shrieking, my son was frightened. He wanted to know who they were and where they were going. I explained the firemen  *were going to help someone put out a fire. Then I decided maybe it would help him if I took him to a firehouse so he could see the men on the truck when all was quiet and there was no loud action. He loved the experience. The firemen were very kind and let him sit in the truck. It was a great day. Now he considers them his friends, and he is not so afraid of the siren now."*

That was the kind of experience that helps a child understand what is going on around him and takes away some of the fear of things unknown. This is part of many nursery-school programs. How many of you have taken such excursions?

"I take my daughter to the library with me. She enjoys going there because there is a children's room where she can pick out books. She decides which ones she wants to borrow and she goes to the counter to check them out with me while I check out mine. She now understands that we keep them a little while and that we can get others when we bring these back. Once in a while there is a story hour for three-year-olds. I have taken her and she seems to enjoy it. Now she knows what a library is and what she can do there."

That not only increases her knowledge about a library, but also gives her an interest in books and reading that may remain with her all her life.

"Our great adventure recently has been the post office. My daughter watches for the postman each morning to see if he will bring a letter from Grandma. I thought it would be a good idea for us to write a letter to Grandma and stamp it and then take it to the post office to mail so Grandma's mailman could bring her a letter. This she found very exciting, and now she knows what Grandma must do to send a letter."

"When I go shopping, I take my daughter. Now she knows that the bakery is where we buy bread and rolls and, occasionally, cookies. She knows the supermarket and where she gets a piece of fruit if she wants something. She is getting to know many of the regular clerks and regards them as friends. Some are pleasant to her and recognize her. I am just wondering what will happen if we meet up with a cross one."

Unpleasant Experiences

"Our routine is somewhat the same. But we did have an unpleasant experience. There was a new clerk in the bakery, and she was quite disorganized and rushed on her first day and didn't say 'hello' to my son or offer a cookie. He began to cry, so I told her the usual procedure and she thrust a cookie in his hand gruffly. On the way home, he kept asking why she didn't want to give him a cookie. I just couldn't think of a good answer so I said maybe next time she would remember—or the old clerk would be back."

It is too bad that not all people treat children—particularly small children—nicely. We would like to protect our children for as long as possible from such experiences. However, when they do occur we should help the child cope with the situation. We can say, for instance, "The clerk was new. She didn't know just what to do. I think next time she will know. We will remind her if she doesn't remember."

"It isn't just grown-ups who can be unpleasant. My daughter plays in the same park playground almost every day. Most of the children are getting

to know each other, but the other day there were two new boys in the sandbox. When she approached enthusiastically, expecting to play as usual, one looked up and said, 'Go away.' Then the other one chimed in 'Go away.' She was upset, and she came running to me crying. I tried to comfort her and looked around for their mother, but there was just a maid who was reading and not paying attention. I went up to the boys and said, 'This sandbox is for everyone to share. It is not your sandbox. She plays here every day, and she can play today. There is room for all of you.' They simply picked up some sand and threw it in my face. I turned to the maid. She looked up in a surly way and said, 'Let them fight it out themselves.' I simply kept still, plunked myself down at the edge of the sandbox, and told my child to play in it all she wanted to. They got the idea; soon they were watching my daughter and trying to help her. Do you think I should have let them 'fight it out' among themselves?"

Children of this age are not ready to advocate for themselves. It is still the parents' job to do it and model for the children the kinds of things to say, as you did.

"One thing I enjoy is the fact that my son can actually converse with me. He makes such surprising comments and asks so many questions. I don't always know how to answer him."

"My daughter does that too. Sometimes she asks a question in a high-pitched voice so everyone can hear on the street. The other day we saw a man walking with the help of a cane in one hand and a kind of crutch in the other. She pointed and said in what seemed to me a very loud voice, 'Mommy, look at the man. Why does he walk like that?' She was very insistent, and I was embarrassed. I explained that he must have hurt his leg and had to walk that way. The first thing she said to her father that night was 'the man must have hurt his leg.' Her father went into more detail and said he must have had an accident and fallen down. That satisfied her more."

Children are often startled by someone who seems strange to them. They will make comments and ask questions, as your daughter did. Before offering an explanation, it may help to ask the child what she thinks or imagines may have happened. In that way you may find out what the child really wants to know. In this instance, your child may have worried whether such a thing could happen to her or anyone she knew and wanted reassurance.

Understanding Family Relationships

"My son is confused by the relationship of one person to another. He is having difficulty understanding that my mother is his grandmother and also the grandmother of my sister's little girl, his cousin. He says, 'No, no, my grandma.' A week ago, when we went to a family gathering, there was a cousin there he had never seen before. My mother had to hold each one on her lap and say, 'I am your grandmother and I am Sally's grandmother.

And you are Sally's cousin and she is your cousin and you are both my grandchildren.' Is it unusual for a child to act that way?"

This is the time that children begin to become aware of relationships. They may need to have these relationships explained to them over and over again. For example, they do not realize until told that Grandma or Grandpa is also Daddy's or Mommy's mother or father. This is indeed a great discovery for children.

"My daughter is going through that now. She understands that Daddy's mother is her grandmother, but she thinks that her friend's grandmother is her grandmother, too."

"My child seems to be trying to get straight who everybody is. He wants to know who their mommy and daddy are, and where they are. At first I thought this strange. Now I can see that it is not just curiosity but trying to understand about people."

These examples show how the children's worlds are expanding. All of the experiences that they have with policemen, postmen, firemen, and grocery clerks help them become better acquainted with the world outside their homes. Helping them to understand is one of the exciting and pleasant aspects of being a parent.

Protecting Your Child

Most parents grew up in an era when children were shielded from learning about unpleasant or dangerous events—especially kidnappings and sexual abuse. Childhood was the age of innocence. Now we are living in a different era. There is an increase in violent crimes. Kidnappings and sexual abuse are frequent events and come very close to many of us. For many children all this horror is as close as the TV set. Parents do not want their children to accept violence as the usual way of life, and at the same time they don't want them to be alarmed and believe that they may become victims. But parents do want to prepare their children to cope if confronted by the threat of harm. With the recent discovery of child abuse in some day-care centers, this is a more pressing issue than ever before.

There has been much discussion recently about the rise of violence, particularly in our own communities. No doubt this has caused you some concern. Have you been thinking how best to protect your children from violence?

"This is a topic that I always tried to avoid. I was brought up to think little children should not have to know about such things. But now I'm not sure. It's happening too often and getting into our own neighborhood."

"You don't have to go outside your house. Violence comes right into your living room on TV. You put on what you think is going to be a benign, safe

program, and before you know it there are fights, bloodshed, and all kinds of frightening things that you don't want your child to see."

This is true. But it is possible to control which programs a child watches. A parent should be watching TV with the child to know what she is exposed to and to be able to turn it off or change channels when necessary.

"What do I do if my child is inadvertently exposed to something that I don't think is right for her? Do I tell her how bad it was, that it was just make-believe, or what?"

The best approach is to try to find out what the child thought about the program, how the child interpreted it, and how real it seemed to her. Then you may have a better idea of what to say to the child.

"Recently, I turned on what I thought was a nice story about a mother and her children. I went to the kitchen to put the dinner in the oven, and when I came back the mother had been shot by an intruder. My child was crying and wanted the TV off. He still doesn't want it on, his sleep pattern has been disturbed, and he clings to me. What should be done?"

How did you handle the situation? What did you say or do?

"I picked him up and held him and turned off the set as soon as I got an idea of what had happened. I said they were just playing, that is wasn't for real, and I took him into the kitchen with me. When he went back into the living room, he looked at the set and stayed close to me and said 'No, no' to the set."

It was good that you picked him up and held him and took him to do something with you. It might have been helpful, too, to ask him what he thought happened and then to be able to tell him it was just a story and not real. He also needed to be reassured that it wasn't happening in his own home, and that you were all right and he was all right. For a few days after an episode in which a child is afraid something may happen to a parent or other member of the family or even himself, it is a good idea to reassure the child. For example, you can mention how well you feel, how well he looks, what a nice day it is, and what good things you are going to do. At bedtime, say what fun the day has been and speak of a pleasant event that will happen the next day.

"What about protecting them from real things that can happen? What I have in mind is kidnapping. How do you prepare a child for such a thing without scaring them to death or even just confusing them?"

Usually, until children are about three, they are very closely watched by the parent or caretaker and are not accessible to strangers. However, children can wander away in parks, shopping centers, or department stores if not strapped in their carriages. So it is necessary, unpleasant as it may seem, to try to warn them not to talk to strangers when mother or another caretaker is not with them. We must remember the level of their language development—how much they can understand and how much they can say—and not give them a lecture. For example, it is sufficient to say, "When Mommy is not with you, don't talk to somebody you don't know."

"I used to think that was okay—until the janitor in a building where a friend lives was accused of kidnapping a child in the building. Nothing bad happened; he was found giving her candy. But it is scary. So now I say, 'Don't talk to anybody if Mommy is not there.' "

"Isn't that interfering with children's socialization? I can just visualize my child sitting in a room with one of my friends while I'm out getting some refreshments and refusing to speak."

Of course it is not an ideal situation, and it does hinder socialization. It also requires much anticipation of events on the part of the parent or other caretaker. To avoid antisocial behavior in the situation you described, you would have to take your child, and perhaps even the guest, to get the refreshments ready so the child would not be confronted with a strange visitor.

"I am glad you always refer to the 'parent or other caretaker,' because I am working outside the home and it is important for me to instruct the caretaker, too."

We are fully aware that many mothers now work outside the home full- or part-time. They do have to depend in these crucial years on other caretakers, and they need to know how to instruct the caretakers about many issues. With reference to the incident of the janitor giving the child candy, another admonition to children is, for example, "We must not take anything from anybody—not candy, a lollipop, a cookie, not anything—unless Mommy [or name the child's caretaker] says you may."

"That is one of the big issues for my child and it worries me. I wonder what I should do if she asks me why? I don't want to say because it may be a bad person who may want to hurt you. I don't think she'd buy it anyway."

At this age, children are beginning to ask "Why?" But an involved explanation may be too much for them to comprehend and result in another "Why?" It is better to say simply but firmly, "That's the way to do it" or "That's the way everyone does it. No one takes things from someone we don't know if Mommy [or the caretaker] doesn't say it is all right to take it." When they are older—say, four or five—they may be able to understand "Because it is dangerous" or "Because they may give you something that isn't for you" or even "Because they may give you something that isn't good for you."

"I'm always afraid that someone will entice my child to go with them to kidnap her for ransom, or to sexually abuse her. I want to protect her but not scare her."

■   ■

We want to shield our children and not make them anxious. We have the impulse to "tell it like it is" in order to protect them, but they are too young to understand. However, they can understand an explanation like "Never go anywhere with anyone even if they give you candy and are nice unless Mommy [or the caretaker] says you may. You must always ask Mommy [or the caretaker] first. All children must do that." It is important to emphasize that this is what all children must do, so it doesn't appear to your child that it applies only to her.

"Recently there have been reports that children have been molested by baby-sitters in their own homes and in day-care centers. What about this problem?"

These are very grave situations. To counter them, parents need first to have the kind of relationship with their children in which they feel free to confide in the parent—and feel the parent will listen and not disbelieve them. In addition, they have to know that they have a right not to let anyone touch their bodies where they do not want to be touched. That means family members and friends as well. Children seem to have a gut feeling when something's not right, but it helps them to know they have parental support. You can say, for example "Remember, you can tell anyone who touches you that you don't want them to touch you and that you don't like it and to stop it. Then you must tell me about it, even if they tell you not to. I'm your mommy, and I need to know all about what you do. That's the best way."

This is certainly a distasteful situation, but in these times precautions need to be taken as sensitively and appropriately as we know how.

"Another situation that bothers me is robbers and burglars entering the house in the guise of a serviceperson. My son likes to run to the door now and can reach the knob to open it. I feel I have to tell him not to open the door for anyone. But how can I tell him that it may be someone who has come to rob us?"

This is another situation that requires a set of precautions, restrictions, and admonitions that are unpleasant for the child. Fortunately, there are some physical precautions that may be taken, such as putting chains on outside doors and installing peepholes. You can also offer a brief explanation, such as "Remember, Mommy has to see who it is before we open the door, for we never open the door unless Mommy [or the caretaker] is there to look out and see who is there. Sometimes we have to ask who it is and what they want."

"I have noticed that you say 'we have to' instead of 'you must.' Why is that?"

"You must . . ." sounds like a command. Children do not respond to commands well. "We . . ." connotes a cooperative effort that children can respond to more easily. All of these efforts we are making to help children protect themselves require unpleasant limitations, and we want as much cooperation and compliance from the children as possible.

The Second Child

Some parents may be planning to have another child now. They may feel that the first child is now more ready to accept a sibling, but they may still not know just what to expect. When the children were not quite two, we discussed the issues involved in having a second child before the first was old enough to be able to express feelings verbally. The children were still too young to have achieved bowel and bladder control, to begin to accept separation, and to socialize with peers and some adults. What are your expectations now that the children are almost three and have achieved some of these goals?

"We waited until now to have our second child because we thought it would be easier for our son to understand what was happening and what to expect when a new baby arrives. He is saying much more and is beginning to tell us how he feels—that he is tired or hungry or wants to play, for example. He understands so much more of what we tell him, so we think we will be able to prepare him for a brother or sister."

"We had our second child when our son was just twenty months old. He was very confused when the new baby came home and he had to wait sometimes for attention. That is my one regret over not waiting longer. I think at times he still has feelings of disbelief that the baby is here to stay."

It is realistic to expect that the children can now understand explanations about the arrival of a new baby. Even more important, they can ask questions that indicate just what their views and expectations are, so parents can help them understand about the baby.

Expectations

"How much can we expect them to tell us?"

For example, if you tell your child that soon you will be going to a hospital and you will bring back a baby, your child may say, "Mommy don't go to hospital." His response indicates that he is troubled by your going away. You can then allay his anxiety about what he is going to be doing while you are away and who is going to take care of him. You can tell him that he can talk to you on the telephone and just when you will be coming home. Some hospitals now allow siblings to visit, so you may be able to tell him that he can come to see you. If this is not possible, just showing him the hospital may take some of the mystery away. If the hospital offers a tour for siblings prior to delivery, he can participate in that. He may come to feel he is a participant in the baby's arrival and not an outsider.

■   ■

"We are going to have a baby in a little over two months. Our daughter will be three and one month. I tried to emphasize the playmate aspect of having a brother or sister. But recently I heard her tell her playmates that she was going to have a brother and that he would play ball with her. Now I know how big she expects the baby to be and that I have to help her understand that it will be a while before they play ball together."

While you are explaining what the baby will be able to do, you can also explain just what she will be able to do with the baby. For example, you can tell her that she can shake a rattle to get his attention and to divert him when crying; that she can help wheel his carriage, sing and talk to him, or assist with the bath by handing you soap, powder, or a towel. This will add to her feeling of importance and belonging. It is better not to list all of these items at once, but to mention them from time to time as the opportunity arises.

Sharing Mother

"One of my friends has a new baby. Her first child is a girl of three. Every time my friend tries to tend to the baby, the girl claims she needs something desperately—anything to take the mother's attention away from the baby. Whatever toy the baby holds or looks at, she wants. I was quite surprised to see such rivalry. I thought that by three children were better able to share."

Children around three years of age are beginning to be able to share toys, usually by taking turns. Sometimes they may be able to share spontaneously with children they know. At other times, they share less readily. However, sharing a parent, particularly the mother, is more difficult and may take a great deal of adjustment on both the parents' and the child's part. One way to deal with this issue is to have the older child involved in the care of the baby in ways that are appropriate for her. When the child's efforts are recognized, she gets a sense of achievement that raises her self-esteem and gives her a sense of accomplishment.

Relating to Baby

"When I was about three and my younger brother was a baby, I told my mother to send him back. I've heard that other children do it too. Is it because they don't know they are related to the baby?"

Most children this age are beginning to understand how members of a family are related to each other. They can recognize grandparents, whom they may see often and for whom they may have developed affection early, and they can understand that aunts and uncles are sisters and brothers of their parents. For most children it is around this same age that they can begin to understand that the new baby is a member of the family and here to stay. A child can be told, for example, that the baby is a sister just as

Aunt Jane is mother's sister. Helping a child unravel these relationships is one of the enjoyable parts of being a parent.

Regression

"My sister's son is a little over three years old. She had a baby girl about a month ago. Her son has been completely toilet trained for about six months, but he began to wet and soil himself a week after the baby came. Is that just to get his mother's attention?"

"A friend of mine has had a problem with her three-and-a-half-year-old daughter ever since she brought her new baby home. Her daughter was completely weaned from the bottle at around two, but now she refuses to drink from a cup. Is it normal for children to go back a step when a new baby comes into the picture? We're expecting a new baby in about six months, and I'd like to be prepared."

Regressions happen frequently when a new baby is brought home. The older child may see the parent shower so much attention upon the baby and feel that he would like to have that attention, too. He is not so far past the time when he was a baby—wearing diapers, using a bottle—and he remembers the comfort and attention that he received. But it is a transitory reaction.

"What do you do to get over it? My sister was very upset and scolded her son and said he was too big a boy for that, but he hasn't stopped. There are scenes each day over this situation."

It is better not to scold the child. That simply adds insult to the injury he feels over having so much attention paid to the baby. He can't understand why it is acceptable for the baby to wet and soil, but it is not acceptable for him to do it. It may help to say something like "I guess you wanted to be a baby again. You used to use a diaper when you were a baby. Now you are a big boy and can use the toilet. The baby can't do that." Then list some of the other things he can do that the baby can't do yet—playing ball or anything else that the child enjoys doing. Then say no more about the incident. If it happens again, change him without reproving or comforting him. When he does use the toilet, acknowledge it and let him know you are pleased that he is your big boy again. Throughout the day, continue to recognize other mature things he can do that the baby cannot. The regression will be overcome more quickly if this approach is used.

"Is it the same with bottles? I'd hate to have to go back to them once my child was weaned."

It is much the same situation. The child may watch the baby being held and cuddled by mother while being fed. That scene may bring back memories for her of being in that blissful state. If the child refuses her cup and requests a bottle, the best approach is to give it to her without comment or cuddling. The child may find that milk doesn't taste so good coming through the rubber nipple and relinquish it after one or two tastes. It may also help to sit with the child, even hold her on the lap, while she drinks from the cup, then refuse to hold her when she drinks from the bottle. Some children want to be breast-fed when observing the baby nurse but when allowed to try it find it is not as pleasant as they remembered and soon give it up. In general, the less fuss made the sooner the regression is overcome.

"I know it is not possible to manage your life so that the older child feels no displacement by the younger child. But what about giving the baby over to the care of a helper and trying to spend as much time as before with the older child? Or is it better to give up the care of the older child to the helper so he will get undivided attention while the mother takes care of the baby?"

Of course, both children need their mother and her consistent care. However, if you have a choice it is probably better for you to spend as much time as you can with the older child and try to keep her routine as normal as possible. If the older child is in a nursery school for part of the day, the mother has exclusive time with the baby then. When the older child is home, the mother can arrange to have some exclusive time with her if there is someone to help with the baby. Each family has to work out an approach that is best for that family. A grandmother or aunt may be glad to mind the baby while the parent spends time with the older child. Or parents can spell each other. Working parents especially need to plan special times which each will devote to the children.

Becoming a Family

"It sounds as though each child needs so much individual attention. How do they ever get to be a family?"

Perhaps we have been focusing too much on how to help the older child after a baby has arrived. One of the ways to achieve that is to involve the older child in play with and care of the baby. Parents have to be careful to present play with the baby and its care as a privilege and a bonus—not an obligation. Presented that way, involvement with the baby's care is more likely to be assumed with pleasure and a sense of heightened self-esteem. That helps draw the family together. Of course, there will be days when everything goes smoothly, and those when they do not.

Grandparents and In-laws

Grandparents play varying roles in the lives of their grandchildren. Some are an important part of the grandchildren's life; others hardly see their grandchildren—because of physical distance or work commitments, for example. What is the relationship between your children and their grandparents?

■   ■

"My parents are dead, and my husband's parents live three thousand miles away. They are too old to travel, and we have not been able to go to visit them. But we talk to them on the phone often and exchange pictures and presents. So my son knows he has grandparents, but that is about it."

"My parents live down the street, and we are in each other's houses part of each day. So the relationship is a close one. My husband's parents live quite far away, so they can visit only once every other week. Our son knows both sets of grandparents and has good relationships with all of them. I suppose that is an unusual situation."

We have hit on two extremes all at once. It is difficult to help a child feel related to grandparents who are so far away, but parents can remind their child that grandparents do exist and care about the child deeply. In the other situation, the child has the good fortune to have two sets of grandparents, and he can spend a lot of time with one set. This gives him the advantages of having an extended family.

"How important is it for a child to have grandparents and to be close to them? I'm asking this because I feel my parents only interfere with the way I want to bring up my child."

"My mother lives with us and is a constant companion and baby-sitter for our child. So no matter how much we differ on some things, the good she does outweighs any occasional disagreement we may have. She gives me a great deal of freedom."

Grandparents Who Baby-sit

"My mother isn't working, but she has six grown children. She says she has done all the baby-sitting she is going to do. No one helped her when her children were little, she says, and all her children will have to do their own baby-sitting just as she did."

"In our case, our son is the only grandchild. My parents and my husband's parents have sort of a rivalry to see who can be the baby-sitter. They urge us to leave our son with them if we want to go away. They are also willing to come to our house. Our son likes them all and has certain things he prefers to do with each. One set are entertainers, so they like to sing and play singing and dancing games. The other set likes to do things such as visit the park and the zoo."

As you have all been saying, families have different needs and ways of doing things. The role of grandparents as baby-sitters is a very important one, especially since good baby-sitters are hard to find and are too expensive for some families. However, grandparents should be permitted other roles with respect to their grandchildren. It is good for children to have other individuals to relate to, with whom they feel secure, whose presence they enjoy, and from whom they can learn. Some grandparents can be models and teachers.

Financial Support

"We needed some financial help after the baby came and I stopped working. Our parents came to our rescue, and we didn't have to ask them. They

knew there would be an increase in expenses so they offered to help. They don't baby-sit, but they do care."

"We've been talking here about grandparents who help in some way. What about when it's the other way round—when you have to help them because they are sick or can't afford to take care of themselves, or both?"

These are both difficult issues—needing either to accept from, or give to, grandparents time, effort, or financial help. These are realities of life, and the way you handle them sets an example for your children. If the parent has to give up too much time and effort to care for a grandparent, the child may come to resent the grandparent. But if the child has established a good relationship with that grandparent, the child may learn compassion for other human beings.

Children's Feelings Toward Grandparents

Let's discuss your children's feelings about their grandparents.

"I hate to say this, but my son is afraid of his grandfather, who is a big, jolly, hearty man with a loud voice. When he comes to visit us, my son cries and clings to me and will not go to him at all. At first that was a disappointment to my father. Now my son is fearful and stands back from him for about an hour. Finally he begins to play with him. Is that an unusual situation?"

Some children need time to size up a visitor, to see if he is friendly and safe to get close to. Large people with loud voices intimidate some children. A grandfather who is an infrequent visitor may be a virtual stranger to the child, and the child must get used to him. The child needs to know that he is not considered to be behaving strangely and that he will not be forced to make contact with grandfather. In time, grandfather and grandson will be friends if the child is supported by understanding parents and the grandfather is helped to understand the child's needs.

"My husband's mother recently had a stroke. She gets around now with the help of a cane, and her speech is not clear. When she comes into a room she makes quite a commotion, and my daughter is afraid of her. My mother-in-law was a very pleasant person before the stroke, and my daughter can't understand what has happened. I hold her hand while I try to help Grandma, and she is beginning to help too. She is beginning to understand that Grandma had a 'boo boo' and we are helping her get better."

How parents deal with a situation sets an example for the child. You showed your child how you helped her disabled grandmother, giving your child support by holding her hand until she followed suit. You helped your daughter overcome her fear by explaining Grandma's condition. It is important that you did not seem upset by Grandma and did not try to avoid having her around. Children's fear is allayed more by the parents' behavior than by any explanation.

■   ■

Interfering with Routine

"My father loves to stop by at night on his way home and play with our son. He gets our son all excited and then leaves. So when Daddy comes home our son is all keyed up and can't settle down for his dinner and bedtime."

"Our daughter can't wait to have her grandparents come. They enjoy each other so much. But when they come, all my discipline goes out the window. With them there are no limits to cookies or candy. No toy is too expensive. There is no limit to her running, and no bedtime. When they leave, it takes her several days to get back to normal."

"We have the same situation. I'm afraid that my child is going to prefer her grandparents to me because I set limits and they don't."

"That is better than a grandparent who is so wrapped up in herself that when she comes to visit she hardly pays attention to the child. My mother-in-law seems to be jealous of the attention we pay our son. She pouts if I have to attend to my son and she has to wait for something."

Indulgent grandparents do not harm the children. The children will not love them more than their parents—just differently. The extra cookie or later bedtime or excited play all make for good memories of childhood and grandparents. However, if it is too upsetting to the parents, it is always possible to talk it over with grandparents in a kindly way and to set up the kind of things and the manner of play they can find acceptable. Most children learn what to expect from grandparents and parents, and they accept the difference.

A grandparent who seems uninterested in her grandchild may change her ways if she is shown how. She may not know how to assume her role as a grandparent. We tend to think grandparents should naturally know how to be grandparents, and we are annoyed if they don't. Some need to be helped to accept and enjoy the role.

"My child loves to have his grandmother tell him stories about what it was like when his father was a little boy and how he behaved. During these sessions, my son is quiet and attentive, and he asks questions. He also wants to know about his aunts and uncles and cousins."

That is a wonderful way for children to learn about their families and family relationships. It is a good experience for the child, and a good way for a grandparent to establish a strong relationship with the child.

Learning About Their Roots

"My father-in-law is quite European in his ways, and he likes to tell our children about how it was 'in the old country.' He tells them stories about different family events, how holidays were celebrated . . . things like that. I think they are learning a lot from him."

■   ■

I am sure you are right. Grandparents make a valuable contribution when they teach children about their cultural heritage and family history.

Religion and Spirituality

Now that the children are becoming more active and participating in more activities with you, have some of you been wondering about the introduction of religion and ethics?

"We've been attending religious services since our daughter was an infant. We had no one to leave her with and since we always attended church we just took her and one of us held her. If she cried, one of us just stepped outside with her."

"We've been doing the same with our son, but now that he is older and active it's difficult to keep him quiet during a whole service. One of us may have to go outside with him."

"At our church there is a baby-sitting service that we use. Once in a while they call on us to come to help, but most of the time it works."

"Our church has set up a play group. The children color books with religious pictures, and around special holidays they learn to sing religious songs. It's geared for young children and is not high pressure at all. The children seem to enjoy it, so we were intending to enter our son as soon as he is three."

"Our church offers a program like that, but it starts with two-year-olds. We tried to have our daughter attend, but she would have none of it. She sometimes stands at the door and watches, but only if one of us is with her. We don't want to leave her there crying, because then she'd probably fuss about going to church with us."

"My husband and I had very little formal religious instruction. We see the pleasure and comfort some of our peers and their families derive from religion. We feel we'd like our child to have that experience. Is it too soon to begin?"

The children are still a little too young for formal religious training. They are not verbal enough; nor do they have the necessary conceptual ability. However, some children may be able to separate from parents long enough to spend time in a play group while the parents are attending service.

"I don't think such young children need formal religious teaching. I think they should be set an example of love and kindness at home, in the way family members talk and act to each other. I wasn't born in this country. In my country the church was mostly for christenings, marriages, and funerals. The real teaching was in the home. That's the way we want it for our son."

"Doesn't each family have to do what they think is right according to the way they were brought up?"

In our country that is the accepted way. However, we are talking about formal religions as they are practiced by different denominations. We are also concerned with ethical issues that are introduced in the home when children are very young and that become the foundation for belief systems.

Belief Systems

"Could you explain belief systems?"

Let's use the example of a mother doing everything in the same order each day for an infant. The infant gets a sense that his day follows a predictable sequence. This helps him develop trust in his mother. When parents are consistently available to fill an infant's needs, the infant establishes trust in them. He has faith that his mother will be there for him. That faith can be the basis for religious faith.

Trust

"Do you mean that the baby's ability to trust his parents makes it possible for him to later have faith in God?"

A child has to be able to trust his parents before he can then trust others. To small children, parents are all-knowing, all-loving, all-powerful beings whom they trust to satisfy their needs. When they grow older they can extend that feeling to a higher power, depending on the religious practices the family embraces.

"This aspect of being a parent was never part of my thinking. Are there other ways that we influence our children in the area of religion?"

Let's take setting limits. From the time a child learns to reach out and touch objects, we stop her if the act is harmful and substitute an approved activity. In other words, we set firm limits on disapproved activities and enthusiastically offer approved ones. The child gradually internalizes a whole catalog of do's and don'ts. In this way she learns to distinguish between the approved and disapproved activities of her society. This experience readies her for later acceptance of religious sanctions.

"We were brought up in a very strict religious denomination. It put fear in our hearts about the least little transgression. Almost everything seemed to be a sin. We don't want that for our child."

If that was your experience and you were not happy with it, you have every right to make a different choice for your child.

Sharing and Caring

"How else do we influence our children's preparation for religious activities? I have in mind spiritual qualities such as loving, sharing, and caring."

Sharing is something that our children are just beginning to achieve. We help them by teaching them to take turns. At this age, they may be able to take turns with a tricycle in the park or share a cookie with friends. If sharing is not forced on them prematurely, it may come easily to them for the rest of their lives.

Parents teach caring by modeling it for their child—by showing love and care for each other and the child, and by demonstrating concern for each other, other members of the family, and friends.

"I can see that all the time when my daughter plays with her dolls. She sets up an exact copy of the way we sound, what we say, and how we react. So I guess that is the way she will treat people when she grows up."

"What about Bible stories? At our church children are told Bible stories during nursery sessions. We aren't sure our child is ready for them yet."

Some children this age are able to listen to longer stories, depending on how much the story is simplified conceptually and how much participation and action is supplied in the telling. Some Bible stories can be frightening to children. Or the stories may be too removed from the children's range of experience to be appreciated. Parents should decide about their own child's readiness and whether the manner of presentation is appropriate for the child.

Belonging to a Group

"Why should a child be burdened with all the trappings of organized religion when the parents can teach them so many fundamentals at home?"

It is true that parents can teach the fundamentals of a belief system at home. However, belonging to a particular religious group also helps a child establish group identity. As she grows, this ability can give her a sense of belonging and of being accepted in a social institution. Some of you have expressed a certain remorse over having missed out on this. Each family must make a decision on this issue in view of family members' background, culture, personalities, and experiences. Each family needs to bear in mind that their decision is right for them and that another family's solution is right for that family. Religion is an emotional and social experience that can remain important throughout the child's life.

Feelings Parenting Evokes

We've spent much time these past months discussing patience, consistency, firmness, creativity, and the many other demands made of parents. So this may be a good time to look at the feelings that parents experience. Some parents may be so busy that they have not even had time to give this subject any thought.

"I was raised in a large family. Children were considered part of the obligation of marriage; raising them was a job like any other. Love meant

■   ■

taking care of us. When my son was born, I stayed home while my wife worked. It was then that my views on child rearing changed. I got such a sense of satisfaction from making him comfortable and seeing him contented after a burp or a little play. That feeling has continued. I suppose my parents felt that way too, but I didn't understand then."

Being a parent can make one more understanding of one's own parents and upbringing.

"I think at first I was scared. The first day my husband went to work and my mother left, there I was a parent, responsible for a human being. Gradually that scared feeling began to lessen, and I began to learn how to notice all the little things the baby did in response to what I did. That got to be fun. I felt I was really learning to be a mother instead of a scared little girl. Now I like the role. I like the job."

"My feelings are very simple. I got my first kick when our baby smiled for the first time. Then I knew I was 'in' as a parent; and ever since, the laughs and hugs make my day. Even if a dozen other things go wrong in the day, that smile makes up for everything."

"I guess I've been what is called a doting father. I can't wait to get home to have my child come running to greet me. We exchange a big hug, and then he wants to play. Finally I get to say hello to my wife, but it seems he comes first now."

"That's the part that used to get to me. When my husband came home and seemed not to pay any attention to me, I felt very jealous. One day we discussed it, and it suddenly dawned on me that I was feeling left out the way I did as a kid when my father paid attention to the new baby after me. Now I enjoy the pleasure my husband and son get from each other."

That experience is common among young mothers, but more often it happens to fathers.

Fathers' Feelings

"I come from a family which by present standards is very old-fashioned. My father got the red-carpet treatment when he came home, and we kids knew it. So I was quite upset after our baby came to see what a back seat I took. The boys at the office who were fathers kidded me about it and set me straight. Then I began to notice more about the baby, and my wife pointed out things about him. He began to be 'our baby,' not just hers, and that makes me feel good. I realize that I no longer feel the need to be waited on by my wife. I get my attention from her and the baby in a different way, because they are so glad to see me when I get home."

"I sometimes try to think back over the three years to what has given me the most joy. I think of the baby's first smile, of course, and the excitement over the first tooth. But the baby's first steps was the most exciting moment by far."

A child's early advances and accomplishments are exciting moments for parents. All parents feel differently about different "firsts."

"The most thrilling part for us now is the talking. We are a very verbal family, and it means so much to have our child able to talk with us. It has been such fun to watch her speech develop. The first word, 'Da, Da,' was such a thrill. Then came 'Mama,' and then so many more words in quick succession. Now she speaks in full sentences, and we feel we have a real person."

"Ever since our baby began to talk, I felt he was more of a person. Now that he can speak in sentences, he is getting to be a real companion. I don't feel so lonesome anymore when we are together."

"Besides the talking, there's the sprouting of ideas. Our child now seems to be making so many more connections. We noticed a while back when he asked where the mailman lived. Before that he knew where we lived and that his grandparents and his little friend lived in different places. Then he became interested in knowing the relationship of one person to another. It was very exciting to watch his mind develop and to help him."

Language and communication are a very important part of a child's development, something that most parents look forward to eagerly. Language is what differentiates man from other animals. It would not happen if parents did not speak to their children and model language. It is one of the important parts of a parent's job and one that can give a parent much pleasure, as some of you have pointed out.

"I think I enjoy most the advances our child is making in talking. I feel we are getting to know and understand him better, and he seems to be learning more about us and the world. I feel now there is more of an opportunity to teach him things and that gives me a feeling of being important and having a real purpose."

The Parent as Teacher

Parents are the child's first teachers, although the role of the parent as a teacher is one that some parents are not always conscious of. The child can learn more from her parents in her first three years than she learns in the rest of her life. Her initial understanding of the world is through her parents.

"I used to worry that I might not be doing the right things as a role model for our child. But as our child reached each milestone—smiling, walking, talking, playing, discovering the world and mostly enjoying it—I began to feel more secure and good about being a parent."

It is interesting to hear you say "mostly enjoying it," because a child's level of happiness is a measure of his development and of how well he is doing overall.

A child is generally thought to be secure and comfortable with himself and his surroundings if he can express joy at his achievements and when, in response to the support of his parents and other aspects of his environment, he is stimulated to explore and achieve more.

"But we can't all be happy with our children all the time. There are times when they need a little discipline, and they are not happy about that."

A child may not be happy at the time that she has to accept some limit to her activity. But in the long run a child whose parents have set consistent limits feels secure and comfortable, because she knows that there are boundaries that she can count on. Usually, a secure child is happy and content.

"Since very early in our son's life we've heard it said that consistent limits lead to a better parent-child relationship and a happier family. In fact, watching him learn to accept limits—beginning with not touching a hot radiator, then not pulling the cat's tail, then holding my hand crossing streets—has given me more satisfaction as a parent than almost anything else."

"I used to think that when I became a parent my children would behave. I thought you just had to order a child severely once and that took care of it. Well, I've learned otherwise. It took a lot of patience and perseverance on our part, but we think our child is pretty well behaved and likable, and that's a pleasure and satisfaction that's very special to us."

Teaching discipline by setting consistent limits while being firm and patient is one of the hardest parts of parenting. Once parents realize that they can achieve this without being police officers to their children, the role becomes very rewarding.

Enjoying New Things

"I've had to become interested in so many new things for my child's sake. I've taken her swimming, taught her arts and crafts, and given her an appreciation for music—all things I've never had time for myself. Although it's still on a very primary level, it's added a different dimension to my life."

"Having a child has made us think harder about the world we are bringing her up in. We've become more involved in what goes on in our community and the political situation. I think we've grown a lot. Maybe it would have come anyway, but having a child seemed to give us an added incentive."

"I have noticed that having my own child has made me more tolerant of and interested in children in general. I care now what happens to children—what kind of world they are inheriting, whether they are happy or not, et cetera. I think I'm a better person for it. It makes life more interesting too."

These are some of the more subtle themes of having children, and I'm glad you are recognizing them. You all seem to be realizing that you play an important role as advocates for children.

"For me the most satisfying part of being a parent is knowing that there is someone who needs me and loves me and whom I love."

"I'm a single parent. It hasn't been easy for me to be breadwinner, teacher, and both parents to my child, but it makes me feel very important and needed, and that makes it all worthwhile for me."

The affectional aspects of being a parent are important for most parents. It is good for a parent to feel needed and for a child to feel secure that there is someone who will always be available to fulfill his or her needs.

It is obvious that different aspects of parenting affect each parent differently. All in all, it is clear from our discussions that being a parent is an important and diverse role that has many rewards.

12

We have come to the end of the three years of the Parenting Program. We have had many discussions and made many discoveries. What do you view as the major developments in these three years?

"As a father who can't spend too much time with his son, I notice most the way he gets around now—how active he is on his tricycle, how much better he runs. He can even throw a ball and sometimes he catches it if you can place it right. Come to think of it, that's the way we have fun together."

"My wife and I both work, so we look forward to our child's exuberant greeting when we come home. She is so happy to see us and follows us around chattering as we change clothes. She's getting to be a friend and companion."

"I'm home most of the time, and I also notice the terrific exuberance about everything. Our daughter is now able to play quite a while, and she is so busy all the time. She moves about so fast that I just can't keep up with her."

"Our son is also exuberant and active. He's a lot of fun, but he is a handful. He has to be watched every minute, I don't know how my wife does it all day. I'm pooped after the weekend."

Some of the children are beginning to be much more active and more exuberant. Although they can play a little longer on their own, they need to be watched carefully, because they are very curious and want to explore new objects and places that may be dangerous.

Judgment

"When can I begin to rely on my child's judgment? I guess what I mean is: How long do I have to be so watchful?"

That question can't be answered specifically. Good judgment comes with maturity and experience, so children acquire it at different stages of development.

Language

"The advance that I find most astonishing and pleasing is the acquisition of language. My child is actually beginning to converse. She picks up everything she hears. The other day she said to our sitter, 'That is not necessary' when the sitter wanted to help her with a toy. I nearly fell over."

"Picking up new words is great, but it has its drawbacks. My daughter was watching her father hammering a nail into the wall. He missed the nail and hit his finger, and he came out with a 'damn.' She has been repeating it every occasion she gets."

Children imitate what they see and hear. As you have discovered, this can result in amusing or embarrassing situations.

"What should a parent do in a situation like that? The first time we were taken by surprise and laughed, but after that it didn't seem very funny."

Sometimes it is helpful to say something like "Daddy didn't mean to say that. It is not a word to say every day." If the child continues to use the offensive word, ignore it. Use of the word will gradually disappear through lack of reinforcement.

New Interests

"Along with the increasing conversation, I like the interest my daughter shows in looking at books and wanting to tell what is in the pictures. We spend a lot of time doing that."

"I find the interest my son has in exploring new situations—the bank, the post office, and, of course, the children's room at the library—has increased. He wants to know what is going on everywhere and who is doing what."

Talking with children, listening to them, reading to them, and taking them on small excursions give them experiences that stimulate their concept formation and increase their interest in and understanding of the world around them. That's a part of parenting that many people find exciting.

"I'm not so involved in areas like bathing and dressing our child, but I can't wait to get home some nights just to hear his new discoveries and ideas."

Socializing

"One thing that is making life a little easier and pleasanter for me is the way my daughter is beginning to behave in her play with other children. She doesn't grab everything the other child has. She is more willing to share or even exchange a toy than she was before. I sometimes hear her say, 'I play with the doll, okay?' "

"I've noticed that too. My son can play amicably with some children for a much longer time. But sometimes it doesn't work that way, and we can't figure it out."

Children have good days and bad days. But you may be noticing that your child plays better with children she knows—a child that she regards as a friend. Problems are more likely to arise with new playmates—children whose ways are not familiar to your child. These situations require a lot of parental involvement and monitoring.

Manners

"I've noticed that my child is beginning to be better about manners. He more often uses a spoon and fork instead of his hands. He sometimes even says 'Hello' and 'Good-bye.'"

"My child is getting better with 'Thank you' and sometimes even 'Please.'"

"I just can't say we are making much progress with manners. I can't seem to make a dent in that area."

"I'm not impatient with my son's lack of manners, but his grandmother reminds me about it and that gets me on edge."

It's natural to want children to make their grandparents happy about their behavior. But we have to bear in mind that grandparents sometimes forget when certain behavior develops. You can say to the grandparent, "We're working on that. He will be doing that pretty soon."

Separation

"I'm so glad to report that, for the past two months, my son has been able to stay overnight at his grandmother's without crying for us or waking in the night."

"Even though we both work, we are now able to come home, play a little with our daughter, and go out for dinner or a movie or just visit without the wailing and tears from her. She doesn't like it, and wants to know when we will be home, but it is usually much easier. We do it quite regularly now, and she is getting used to the routine."

Most of the children are showing a great deal of progress with separation, but some may not be able to separate easily and comfortably even at three. Even children age five or six and older are reluctant to separate at times. They need support and reassurance, not disapproval.

Toilet Training

"My child is now toilet trained. He just decided he was ready and asked to be taken to the bathroom. He had good control in just a couple of days. I was so surprised and pleased."

"My child has achieved control during the day, but occasionally at night she has an accident. So we still use diapers at night."

Achieving bowel and bladder control is a big concern for most parents. In this area, as in others, children have their own timetables of readiness.

Most are ready around age three—but that is not a magic number. Control is achieved by some children well before three and by others well after. Parents should never try to force toilet training on a child.

Sleep

"My son used to wake several times a night and come into our room, but that has stopped almost entirely. When it does happen, it is usually when there is some change in routine coming up—a business trip or a vacation, for instance."

The Final Bottle

"My daughter still has a bottle at bedtime. I'll be so glad when she gives it up. She drinks perfectly well from a cup."

"My son had given up bottles on his own by the time he was two and a half. But when our daughter was born three months ago, he watched her having one and decided he needed bottles, too. I had been warned, so it didn't upset me. It lasted about a week; now he is back to cups for his milk and juice."

Giving up the bottle is harder for some children than it is for others. When they are ready, most children give up bottles on their own; others need a little more support. Some give them up when they start nursery school and become busy with more mature activities. A few may be made anxious by nursery school or another change in routine and may cling to a bottle for a sense of security. As we have said so often, the speed with which your child achieves bowel and bladder control and relinquishes bottles are not the achievements by which you should measure success as a parent.

Accepting Limits

"Our biggest achievement is that our child has learned to accept some limits when we set them consistently. We are no longer always saying, 'No, don't do that. Let's do it this way.' We have gotten him to close the refrigerator door, not slam doors, and not run across the street. Just that has made life so much more comfortable."

"Achieving discipline without having to yell has been the hardest part for us."

"Setting limits by being firm and consistent without losing my temper— that's the hardest part of parenting for me. My husband manages better— or at least it seems to me that it is easier for him to be consistent."

I agree that it is hard. But it is also one of the most important issues of parenting. As we have pointed out before, it is an important part of the process of learning what is and is not acceptable behavior in our society. It is the basis for the development of a conscience later on. It is an ongoing issue for parents, because new and different limits are needed as the child grows. Parents who have achieved the ability to be firm and consistent without being harsh will find that this approach continues to be useful.

Preview of the Fourth Year

Let's preview what is in store in the coming year. The children will be able to play longer and share better, but not always. They will continue to be exuberant, at times even boisterous. There will be a big jump in their attention span and their cognitive ability. Some of their questions will be probing and difficult to answer. Their imaginations will flourish. It should be a very exciting and enjoyable time for all of you.

Coming to the end of these parenting sessions has its rewards. You can all look back on days when comforting, changing, feeding, and burping a baby were your main concerns and you felt so inadequate. But look at your children now. They can walk, run, jump, and climb. They can now communicate, express ideas, and socialize. They are learning to accept limits. They are beginning to tell right from wrong, and beginning to have manners. They are able to separate better. They are more aware of the needs and views of others. Many are toilet trained or about to be. They are happy and competent children. This progress is due in great part to your ability to care for them. You can all be very proud of your achievement.

You have a good foundation in parenting. You will be able to use the policies of dealing with physical activity, discipline, judgment, socialization, separation, communication, and support throughout your children's lives.

Suggested Books for Children
Twenty-four to Thirty-six Months

The verbal ability and concentration of children expand greatly between twenty-four and thirty-six months. The books on the following list vary from cloth and cardboard books with few or no words to paper books with simple story lines. If a child shows impatience or restlessness while looking at a particular book, the parent should try a different one. Children may have quite different interests, even at this early age, and the age at which each will enjoy a particular book will vary as well.

Parents and children can make their own books of pictures cut from magazines and pasted on cardboard. Children also enjoy looking at albums of photographs of themselves and hearing stories about themselves.

Adams, George, and Henning, Paul. *First Things*. New York: Platt and Munk.
At the Table; Going for a Ride; In the House; Trucks. 1981. Los Angeles: Price/Stern/Sloan *(cardboard)*.
Baby's First Book. New York: Platt and Munk *(cardboard or cloth)*.
Barton, Byron. 1986. *Trucks; Boats*. New York: Thomas Y. Crowell.
Battagna. Aurelius. 1976. *Come Walk with Me; I Look Out My Window; This Is My House; Let's Go Shopping; A Trip to the Zoo*. New York: Playskool Manufacturing Company (recommended by Pushaw, 1976).
The Bear; The Crane; The Train. 1979. Copenhagen: Carlsen *(cardboard, no words)*.
Bonforte, Lisa. *Baby Animals*. New York: Golden Press *(cardboard)*.
Boynton, Sandra. 1982. *The Going to Bed Book*. New York: Little Simon.
Bridewell, Norman. 1963. *Clifford, the Big Red Dog*. New York: Scholastic.
Brown, Margaret Wise. 1947. *Good Night Moon*. New York: Harper & Row.
———. 1950. *A Child's Good Night Book*. New York: Scott
———. 1952. *The Duck*. Photographs by Ylla. New York: Harper & Row.
Bruna, Dick. *Dick Bruna's Animal Book*. London: Methuen Books *(cardboard)*.
———. *Miffy at the Zoo; Miffy's Birthday*. London: Methuen Books.
———. *My Meals*. A Dick Bruna Zig Zag Book. London: Methuen Books *(cardboard)*.
Burningham, John. 1974. *The Rabbit*. New York: Thomas Y. Crowell.
———. 1975. *The Baby*. New York: Thomas Y. Crowell.
———. 1975. *The Blanket*. New York: Thomas Y. Crowell.
———. 1976. *The Cupboard*. New York: Thomas Y. Crowell.
Cellini, Joseph. 1958. *ABC*. New York: Grosset and Dunlap *(cardboard)*.

Crews, Donald. 1978. *Freight Train.* New York: Morrow.
———. 1980. *Truck.* New York: Greenwillow Books.
Dunn, Phoebe. 1987. *Busy, Busy Toddlers.* New York: Random House.
Ets, Marie Hall. *Play with Me; Just Like Me.* New York: Viking.
Federico, Helen. 1960. *ABC.* New York: Golden *(cardboard).*
A First Book in My Garden; A First Book in My Kitchen. 1980. "Object Lesson" series. England: Brimax Books *(cardboard).*
Flack, Marjorie. *Angus and the Cat; Angus and the Ducks.* New York: Doubleday.
Fujikama, Gyo. 1963. *Babies.* New York: Grosset and Dunlap *(cardboard).*
Gay, Zhenya. *Look!* New York: Viking.
The Golden Fire Engine Book. New York: Golden Press *(cardboard).*
Johnson, John E. *The Sky Is Blue; The Grass Is Green.* New York: Random House *(cloth).*
Kalan, Robert. 1979. *Blue Sea.* New York: Morrow.
Kessler, Ethel and Leonard. *Do Baby Bears Sit on Chairs?* New York: Doubleday.
Krauss, Ruth. 1945. *The Carrot Seed.* New York: Harper & Row.
———. 1948. *Bears.* New York: Harper & Row.
———. 1949. *The Happy Day.* New York: Harper & Row.
Kunhardt, Dorothy. *Pat the Bunny.* New York: Western.
———. *Tickle the Pig.* New York: Golden.
———. 1984. *Pat the Cat.* New York: Golden.
Lenski, Lois. *Davy's Day.* Henry Z. Walck.
———. *Now It's Fall.* Henry Z. Walck.
———. *I Like Winter.* Henry Z. Walck.
McNaught, Harry. 1976. *Baby Animals.* New York: Random House *(cardboard).*
———. 1976. *Trucks.* New York: Random House.
———. 1979. *Trucks.* New York: Random House.
Matthiesen, Thomas. 1968. *Things to See.* New York: Platt and Munk.
Miller, J. P. 1976. *Big and Little.* New York: Random House *(cardboard).*
———. *Farmer John's Animals.* New York: Random House *(cardboard).*
My First Toys. New York: Platt and Munk.
Najaka, Marlies Merk. 1980. *City Cat; Country Cat.* New York: McGraw-Hill *(cardboard).*
Nursery Rhymes. 1979. New York: Random House *(cardboard).*
Oxenbury, Helen. 1982. *Beach Day; Good Night, Good Morning; Monkey See, Monkey Do; Mother's Helper; Shopping Trip.* New York: Dial Press *(cardboard, no words).*
———. 1981. *Friends.* New York: Simon and Schuster.
Pfloog, Jan. 1977. *Kittens.* New York: Random House *(cardboard).*
———. 1979. *Puppies.* New York: Random House *(cardboard).*
Pickett, Barbara, and Kovacs, D. 1981. *The Baby Strawberry Book of Pets.* New York: McGraw-Hill *(cardboard).*
———. 1981. *The Baby Strawberry Book of Baby Farm Animals.* New York: McGraw-Hill *(cardboard).*
Rey, H. A. *Anybody at Home?; Feed the Animals; See the Circus; Where's My Baby?* Boston: Houghton-Mifflin.

Rice, Eve. 1977. *Sam Who Never Forgets.* New York: Morrow.

Richter, Mischa. 1978. *Quack?* New York: Harper & Row.

Risom, Ole. 1963. *I Am a Bunny.* New York: Golden Press *(cardboard).*

Scarry, Patsy. *My Teddy Bear Book.* New York: Golden Press.

Scarry, Richard. 1976. *Early Words.* New York: Random House.

———. 1967. *Egg in the Hole Book.* Racine, Wis.: Western.

———. 1990. *Just Right Word Book.* New York: Random House.

Schlesinger, Alice. 1959. *Baby's Mother Goose.* New York: Grosset and Dunlap *(cardboard).*

Seiden, Art. 1962. *Kittens; Puppies.* New York: Grosset and Dunlap *(cardboard).*

"Show Baby" Series: *Bathtime; Bedtime; Mealtime; Playtime.* 1973. New York: Random House *(cardboard).*

Skarr, Grace. 1968. *What Do the Animals Say?* New York: Young Scott Books.

Steiner, Charlotte. *My Bunny Feels Soft.* New York: Alfred A. Knopf.

The Tall Book of Mother Goose. New York: Harper & Row.

Tensen, Ruth M. *Come to the Farm.* Chicago: Reilly and Lee.

Things That Go. New York: Platt and Munk *(cloth).*

Walley, Dean. *Pet Parade.* Kansas City: Hallmark Cards *(cardboard).*

———, and Cunningham, Edward. *Zoo Parade.* Kansas City: Hallmark Cards *(cardboard).*

Wells, Rosemary. *Max's First Word; Max's Ride; Max's Toys.* New York: Dial *(cardboard).*

———. 1985. *Max's Birthday; Max's Breakfast; Max's Bath.* New York: Dial *(cardboard).*

Wikland, Ilon. *See What I Can Do.* New York: Random House.

Wilkin, Eloise. 1981. *Rock-A-Bye, Baby.* New York: Random House. *(Simple games with rhymes to play with toddlers.)*

Williams, Garth. *Baby Animals.* New York: Western.

———. *Baby's First Book.* New York: Platt and Munk *(cardboard or cloth).*

———. *The Chicken Book.* New York: Delacorte.

Witte, Pat, and Witte, Eve. *The Touch Me Book.* New York: Western.

———. *Who Lives Here?* New York: Western.

Wolde, Gunilla. *This Is Betsy.* New York: Random House *(series).*

Woodcock, Louise. *This Is the Way Animals Walk.* W. R. Scott.

Wynne, Patricia. 1977. *The Animal ABC.* New York: Random House *(cardboard).*

Zaffo, George. *The Giant Nursery Book of Things That Go.* Garden City, N.Y.: Doubleday.

Bibliography

Note: Titles preceded by an asterisk (*) are especially recommended for parents.

Abrahamson, David. 1969. *Emotional Care of Your Child.* New York: Trident Press.

Ainsworth, Mary D. Salter. 1965. Further research into the adverse effects of maternal deprivation. In *Child Care and Growth of Love,* 2d ed., ed. John Bowlby, 191–241. Harmondsworth, England: Penguin Books.

————. 1967. *Infancy in Uganda: Infant Care and the Growth of Attachment.* Baltimore: The Johns Hopkins University Press.

————. 1969. Object relations, dependency, and attachment: A theoretical review of the infant-mother relationship. *Child Development* 40:969–1025.

Ainsworth, Mary D. Salter, and Bell, Sylvia M. 1972. Attachment, exploration, and separation: Illustrated by behavior of one-year-olds in a strange situation. In *Readings in Child Development,* eds. Irving B. Weiner and David Elkind. New York: John Wiley & Sons.

*Ames, Louise Bates, and Chase, Joan Ames. 1973. *Don't Push Your Preschooler.* New York: Harper & Row.

Anglund, Sandra. 1968. Here, even infants go to school. *Today's Health.* March, 52–57.

Auerbach, Alice S. 1968. *Parents Learn Through Discussion.* New York: John Wiley & Sons.

Badger, Earladeen D. 1972. A mother's training program. *Children Today* (U.S. Department of Health, Education and Welfare) 1/3:7–11, 35.

Bayley, Nancy. 1940. Mental growth in young children. *Yearbook of the National Society for the Study of Education* 39/2:11–47.

————. 1969. *Bayley Scales of Infant Development.* New York: Psychological Corporation.

Beadle, Muriel. 1970. *A Child's Mind.* New York: Doubleday.

Bel Geddes, Joan. 1974. *How to Parent Alone: A Guide for Single Parents.* Somers, Conn.: Seabury Press.

Bell, Richard Q. 1971. Stimulus control of parent or caretaker behavior by infant. *Developmental Psychology* 4:63–72.

Bell, Sylvia M., and Ainsworth, Mary D. Salter. 1972. Infant crying and maternal responsiveness. *Child Development* 44:1171–90.

Bernstein, B. 1964. Aspects of language and learning in the genesis of the social process. In *Language in Culture and Society: A Reader in Linguistics and Anthropology,* ed. D. Hymes, 251–63. New York: Harper & Row.

Bettleheim, Bruno. 1962. *Dialogues with Mothers.* New York: Free Press.

Bijou, S. W. 1970. *Experiences and the Processes of Socialization.* New York: Academic Press.

Birch, Herbert G. 1970. *Disadvantaged Children: Health, Nutrition, and School Failure.* New York: Harcourt, Brace & World.

Blank, M. 1964. Some maternal influences on infants' rate of sensorimotor development. *Journal of the American Academy of Child Psychiatry* 3:668–87.

Bloom, Benjamin S. 1964. *Stability and Chance in Human Characteristics.* New York: John Wiley & Sons.

Bowlby, John. 1951. *Maternal Care and Mental Health: Report to World Health Organization.* New York: Columbia University Press.

––––––. 1958. Nature of a child's tie to his mother. *International Journal of Psychoanalysis* 39:350–73.

––––––. 1960. Grief and mourning in infancy and early childhood. In *The Psychoanalytic Study of the Child.* New York: International Universities Press.

––––––. 1969–1980. *Attachment and Loss.* 3 vols. (*Attachment; Separation, Anxiety and Anger;* and *Loss, Sadness and Depression*). New York: Basic Books.

*Brazelton, T. Berry. 1969. *Infants and Mothers.* New York: Delacorte.

*––––––. 1974. *Toddlers and Parents.* New York: Delacorte.

––––––. 1984. *To Listen to a Child.* Reading, Mass.: Addison-Wesley.

Bresnahan, Jean L., and Blum, William. 1971. Chaotic reinforcement: A socioeconomic leveler. *Developmental Psychology* 4:89–92.

Brim, Orville G., Jr. 1961. Methods of educating parents and their evaluation. In *Prevention of Mental Disorders in Children,* ed. G. Caplan, 122–41. New York: Basic Books.

––––––. 1965. *Education for Child Rearing.* Reprint. New York: Free Press.

Brody, Grace F. 1969. Maternal childrearing attitudes and child behavior. *Developmental Psychology* 1:66.

Brody, Sylvia, 1956. *Patterns of Mothering.* New York: International Universities Press.

Bronfenbrenner, Urie. 1970. *Two Worlds of Childhood.* New York: Russell Sage Foundation.

Bruner, Jerome S. 1968. *Processes of Cognitive Growth: Infancy.* Worcester, Mass.: Clark University Press.

*Calderone, Mary S. M.D., and Ramsay, James W., M.D. 1982. *Talking with Your Child About Sex: Questions and Answers for Children from Birth to Puberty.* New York: Random House.

Caldwell, Bettye M. 1972. What does research teach us about day care for children under three? *Children Today* (U.S. Department of Health, Education and Welfare) 1/1:6–11.

Caldwell, Bettye M., and Ricciuti, N. N., eds. 1973. *Review of Child Development Research.* Vol. 3 of *Child Development and Social Policy.* Chicago: University of Chicago Press.

Call, Justin; Galenson, Eleanor; and Tyson, Robert L. 1984. *Basic Books.* Vol. 2. New York: Brunner/ Mazel.

■   ■

*Caplan, Frank, ed. 1971. *The First Twelve Months of Life*. Princeton, N.J.: Edcom Systems, Inc.

Caplan, Gerald, ed. 1961. *Prevention of Mental Disorders in Children*. New York: Basic Books.

Chess, Stella, M.D., and Thomas, Alexander, M.D. 1984. *Origins of Evolution of Behavior Direction*. New York: Brunner/ Mazel.

———. 1980. *Dynamics of Psychological Development*. New York: Brunner/ Mazel.

*Church, Joseph. 1973. *Understanding Your Child from Birth to Three: A Guide to Your Child's Psychological Development*. New York: Random House.

Clausen, John A., ed. 1968. *Socialization and Society*. Boston: Little, Brown.

*Comer, James, and Poussaint, Alvin. 1975. *Black Child Care*. New York: Stratford Press.

Cook, Thomas, D., et al. 1975. *"Sesame Street" Revisited*. New York: Russell Sage Foundation.

Crandall, Virginia. 1972. Achievement behavior in your children. In *Readings in Child Development*, eds. Irving B. Weiner and David Elkind. New York: John Wiley & Sons.

Danziger, Kurt. 1971. *Socialization*. Reprint. Harmondsworth, England: Penguin Books.

Deutsch, Martin. 1960. *Minority Group and Class Status as Related to Social and Personality Factors in Scholastic Achievement*. Ithaca, N.Y.: Society for Applied Anthropology.

———. 1964. Facilitating development in the preschool child: Social and psychological perspectives. *Merrill-Palmer Quarterly* 10:249–63.

———. 1965. The role of social class in language development and cognition. *American Journal of Orthopsychiatry* 35/1:78–88.

Dittman, Laura, ed. 1968. *Early Child Care*. New York: Atherton Press.

*Dodson, Fitzhugh. 1974. *How to Father*. New York: New American Library.

Ende, Robert N. 1983. *Rene A. Spitz: Ideologies from Infancy*. Selected Papers. New York: International Universities Press, Inc.

Erikson, Erik H. 1963. *Childhood and Society*. 2d ed. Reprint. New York: W. W. Norton.

Escalona, Sibylle. 1968. *Roots of Individuality*. Chicago: Aldine Publishing.

Fantz, R. 1963. Pattern vision in newborn infants. *Science* 140:296–97.

Foss, B. N., ed. 1968. *Determinants of Infant Behavior IV*. New York: John Wiley & Sons.

*Fraiberg, Selma H. 1959. *The Magic Years*. New York: Charles Scribner & Sons.

———. 1977. *Every Child's Birthright: In Defense of Mothering*. New York: Basic Books.

*Galinsky, Ellen, and Hooks, William H. 1977. *The New Extended Family: Day Care That Works*. Boston: Houghton-Mifflin.

Garmezy, Norma, and Ritter, Michael. 1985. *Stress of Coping and Development in Children*. New York: McGraw-Hill.

Garvey, Catherine. 1977. *Play*. Cambridge: Harvard University Press.

*Gesell, Arnold L. 1940. *The First Five Years of Life*. New York: Harper & Row.

■   ■

_____. 1943. *Infant and Child Care in the Culture of Today.* New York: Harper & Row.

Gesell, Arnold L., and Amatruda, Catherine. 1947. *Developmental Diagnosis.* 2d ed. New York: Paul B. Hoeber.

*Glickman, Beatrice M., and Springer, Nesha B. 1978. *Who Cares for the Baby? Choices in Child Care.* New York: Schocken Books.

Goldstein, Joseph; Freud, Anna; and Solnit, Albert J. 1973. *Beyond the Best Interests of the Child.* Reprint. New York: Free Press.

Goslin, D. A., ed. 1969. *Handbook of Socialization Theory and Research.* New York: Rand-McNally.

*Green, Martin I. 1976. *A Sigh of Relief: The First-Aid Handbook for Childhood Emergencies.* New York: Bantam Books.

Greenspan, Stanley I., M.D. 1981. *Psychopathology and Adaptation in Infancy and Early Childhood.* New York: International Universities Press.

Greenspan, Stanley I., M.D., and Pollock, George H., eds. 1989, 1990. *The Course of Life.* Vols. 1 and 2. of *Infancy.* Madison, Conn.: International Universities Press.

Harlow, H. 1949. The formation of learning sets. *Psychological Review* 56:51–65.

Hawke, Sharryl, and Knox, David. 1977. *One Child by Choice.* Englewood Cliffs, N.J.: Prentice-Hall.

Healy, Jane M. 1987. *You Child's Growing Mind.* New York: Doubleday.

Hellmuth, Jerome, ed. 1970. *Cognitive Studies.* Vol. 1. New York: Brunner/ Mazel.

Hess, R., and Shipman, V. 1965. Early experience and cognitive modes. *Child Development* 36:869.

*Hoffman, Dale. 1979. A guide to pre-nursery schools. *New York* magazine, October 15.

Hunt, J. McV. 1961. *Intelligence and Experience.* New York: Ronald Press.

_____. 1971. Parent and child centers: Their basis in the behavioral and educational sciences. *American Journal of Orthopsychiatry* 41/1:13–38.

Johnson, Dale L., et al. 1974. The Houston parent-child development center: A parent education program for Mexican-American families. *American Journal of Orthopsychiatry* 44/1:121–28.

Kagan, Jerome. 1971. *Change and Continuity in Infancy.* New York: John Wiley & Sons.

Kagan, Jerome. 1984. *The Nature of the Child.* New York: Basic Books.

Kagan, Jerome; Kearsley, Richard B.; and Zelazo, Phillip R. 1978. *Infancy: Its Place in Human Development.* Cambridge: Harvard University Press.

Katz, I. 1967. The socialization of academic motivation in minority group children. In *Nebraska Symposium in Motivation,* ed. D. Levine, 133–91. Lincoln, Neb.: University of Nebraska Press.

Kessler, Jane W. 1970. Contributions of the mentally retarded toward a theory of cognitive development. In *Cognitive Studies,* ed. J. Hellmuth, vol. 1, 111–209. New York: Brunner/Mazel.

_____. 1966. *Psychopathology of Childhood.* Englewood Cliffs, N.J.: Prentice-Hall.

Knobloch, Hilda, and Pasamanic, Benjamin, eds. 1974. *Gesell and Amatru-*

■   ■

da's Developmental Diagnosis. 3d ed. Hagerstown, MD.: Harper & Row Medical.

Levy, David M. 1956. *Maternal Overprotection.* Reprint. New York: W. W. Norton.

Lewis, M. M. 1963. *Language, Thought, and Personality in Infancy and Childhood.* New York: Basic Books.

―――. 1976. *Origins of Intelligence: Infancy and Early Childhood.* New York: Plenum Press.

*Lidz, Theodore, 1968. *The Person: His Development Through the Life Cycle.* New York: Basic Books.

*Lief, Nina R., and Fahs, Mary Ellen. 1991. *The First Year of Life.* New York: Walker and Company.

* ―――. 1991. *The Second Year of Life.* New York: Walker and Company.

Lief, Nina R., and Zarin-Ackerman, Judith. 1976. The effectiveness of a curriculum of parent education on a group of risk and non-risk mothers and infants. Paper presented at meeting of the American Association of Psychiatric Services for Children, 11 November 1976, San Francisco, California.

Lipsitt, L. 1966. Learning process of human newborns. *Merrill-Palmer Quarterly* 12:45–71.

Litman, Frances. 1969. Environmental influences on the development of abilities. Excerpted from a Harvard Graduate School of Education Pre-School Project Paper presented at the Biennial Meeting of the Society for Research in Child Development, Santa Monica, California.

McClelland, D., et al. 1953. *The Achievement Motive.* New York: Appleton-Century-Crofts, Inc.

McGurk, Harry, 1974. Visual perception in young infants. In *New Perspectives in Child Development,* ed. Brian Foss. Baltimore, Md.: Penguin Books.

Madden, John; Levenstein, Phyllis; and Levenstein, Sidney. 1976. Longitudinal I.Q. outcomes of the mother-child home program—Verbal Interaction Project. *Child Development* 47/4:1015–25.

Mahler, Margaret S., and La Perriere, K. 1965. Mother-child interaction during separation. *Psychoanalytical Quarterly* 34:483–98.

Mahler, Margaret S.; Pine, Fred; and Bergman, Ami. 1975. *The Psychological Birth of the Human Infant—Symbiosis and Individuation.* New York: Basic Books.

Malone, Charles A. 1967. Psychosocial characteristics of the children from a development viewpoint. In *The Drifters,* ed. E. Pavenstedt, 105–24. Boston: Little, Brown.

*Marzollo, Jean. 1977. *Supertot: Creative Learning Activities for Children One to Three and Sympathetic Advice for their Parents.* New York: Harper Colophon Books.

Morris, Ann G., 1974. Conducting a parent education program in a pediatric clinic playroom. *Children Today* 3/6:11–14.

Murphy, Lois B. 1962. *The Widening World of Childhood.* New York: Basic Books.

―――. 1963. Problems in recognizing emotional disturbances in children. *Child Welfare,* Dec., 473–87.

■   ■

Neubauer, Peter B. 1968, The third year: The two-year-old. In *Early Child Care,* ed. L. Dittman, 57–67. New York: Atherton Press.

Newson, Elizabeth, and Newsom, John. 1968. *Four-Year-Olds in an Urban Community.* Chicago: Aldine Publishing.

*Parke, Ross D. 1981. *Fathers.* Cambridge: Harvard University Press.

Pavenstedt, Eleanor. 1965. A comparison of childrearing environments of upper lower and very-low lower class families. *American Journal of Orthopsychiatry* 35:89.

———. 1967. *The Drifters.* Boston: Little, Brown.

Piaget, Jean. 1950. *The Psychology of Intelligence.* New York: Harcourt, Brace.

———. 1970. The stages of the intellectual development of the child. In *Readings in Child Development and Personality,* 2d ed., eds. Paul H. Mussen, John J. Conger, and Jerome Kagan, 291–98. New York: Harper & Row.

Pine, Fred. 1971. On the separation process: Universal trends and individual differences. In *Separation-Individuation: Essays in Honor of Margaret S. Mahler,* eds. John B. McDivitt and Calvin F. Settlage, 113–30. New York: International Universities Press.

*Price, Jane. 1980. *How to Have a Child and Keep Your Job: A Candid Guide for Working Parents.* New York: Penguin Books.

Pringle, M. L. Kellmer, et al. 1967. *11,000 Seven-Year-Olds.* New York: Humanities Press.

Provence, S., and Litman, R. C. 1962. *Infants in Institutions.* New York: International Universities Press.

*Pulaski, Mary Ann Spencer. 1978. *Your Baby's Mind and How It Grows: Piaget's Theory for Parents.* New York: Harper & Row.

*Pushaw, David R. 1976. *Teach Your Child to Talk.* Fairfield, N.J.: CEBCO Standard Publishing.

Rice, Phillip. 1979. *The Working Mother's Guide to Child Development.* Englewood Cliffs, N.J.: Prentice-Hall.

Rowland, L. W. 1948. A first evaluation of Pierre the Pelican. Health Pamphlets, Louisiana Mental Health Studies, no. 1. New Orleans: Louisiana Society for Mental Health.

*Salk, Lee. 1971. *What Every Child Would Like His Parents to Know.* New York: David McKay Co.

Sarbin, Theodore R., and Allen, Vernon L. 1968. Role theory. In *Handbook of Social Psychology.,* 2d ed., eds. Gardner Lindzey and Elliot Aronson, vol. 1, 488–567. Reading, Mass.: Addison-Wesley.

Schaefer, Earl S. 1970. Need for early and continuing education. In *Education of the Infant and Young Child,* ed. V. H. Denenberg. New York: Academic Press.

Sears, Robert R.; Maccoby, E. E.; and Levin, H. 1975. *Patterns of Childrearing.* New York and Evanston, Ill.: Row, Peterson.

Shapiro, David. 1981. *Autonomy and Rigid Character.* New York: Basic Books.

*Singer, Dorothy; Singer, Jerome; and Zuckerman, Diana M. 1981. *Teaching Television: How to Use TV to Your Child's Advantage.* New York: The Dial Press.

■   ■

Skinner, B. F. 1953. *Science and Human Behavior.* New York: Macmillan.

Smith, M. Brewster. 1968. Competence and socialization. In *Socialization and Society,* ed. J. A. Clausen, 270–320. Boston: Little, Brown.

Spitz, Rene A. 1945. Hospitalism and inquiry into the genesis of psychiatric conditions of early childhood. *Psychoanalytic Study of the Child* 1:53–74.

———. 1965. *The First Year of Life.* New York: International Universities Press.

*Spock, Benjamin. 1981. *Baby and Child Care.* New York: Pocket Books.

Steinfels, Margaret O'Brien. 1973. *Who's Minding the Children? The History and Politics of Day Care in America.* New York: Simon & Schuster.

Stern, Daniel. 1988. *The Interpersonal World of the Infant.* New York: Basic Books.

*Stone, Joseph, and Church, Joseph. 1968. *Childhood and Adolescence.* New York: Random House.

Talbot, Nathan B.; Kagan, Jerome; and Eisenberg, Leon. 1971. *Behavioral Science in Pediatric Medicine.* Philadelphia: Saunders.

Terman, Lewis M., and Merrill, M. 1972. *Stanford-Binet Intelligence Scale. Form L-M.* 3d revision. Boston: Houghton-Mifflin.

*Thomas, Alexander; Chess, Stella; and Birch, Herbert G. 1968. *Temperament and Behavior Disorders in Children.* New York: New York University Press.

———. 1977. *Temperament and Development.* New York: Brunner/Mazel.

Weinraub, Marsha, and Lewis, Michael. 1977. *The Determinants of Children's Responses to Separation.* Monographs of the Society for Research in Child Development, no. 172.

*Weiss, Robert S. 1979. *Going It Alone: The Family Life and Social Situation of the Single Parent.* New York: Basic Books.

White, Burton L. 1970. Child development research: An edifice without foundation. In *Readings in Child Development and Personality,* 2d ed., eds. P. H. Mussen et al., 97–117. New York: Harper & Row.

*———. 1975. *The First Three Years of Life.* Englewood Cliffs, N.J.: Prentice-Hall.

White, Burton L., and Watts, Jean Carew. 1973. *Experience and Environment,* Vol. 1. Englewood Cliffs, N.J.: Prentice-Hall.

Wilson, Ronald S. 1972. Twins: early mental development. *Science* 175/4024:914–17.

Winnicott, D. W. 1951. *Transitional Objects and Transitional Phenomena: A Study of the First Not-Me Possession.* In *Collected Papers.* New York: Basic Books.

Work, Henry H. 1972. Parent-child centers: a working reappraisal. *American Journal of Orthopsychiatry* 42/4:582–95.

Yarrow, Leon J. 1968. Conceptualizing the early environment. In *Early Child Care,* ed. L. Dittman. New York: Atherton Press.

Zambrana, Ruth E.; Hurst, Martha; and Hite, Rodney. 1979. The working mother in contemporary perspective: A review of the literature. *Pediatrics* 64/6:862–70.

Zigler, Edward, and Child, Irvin L. 1969. Socialization. In *Handbook of Social Psychology,* 2d ed., eds. Gardner Lindzey and Elliott Aronson, vol. 3, 450–589. Reading, Mass.: Addison-Wesley.

■   ■

Index

■   ■

■   ■